I0145108

My Yoga Journey

The 200-Hour Instructor's Course
That led to Health, Knowledge, Wisdom and Serenity

Lisa Sherman

North Cove Press
PO Box 213
East Greenwich, RI
northcovepress.com

My Yoga Journey
Copyright © 2018 by Lisa Sherman

All rights reserved, including the right of reproduction
in whole or in part in any form, except for the media wishing to quote
brief passages in connection with a review.

My Yoga Journey was written by Lisa Sherman
in partnership with Bob Sherman

ISBN 978-0-9995436-3-4

Library of Congress Control Number 2018912045

Printed and bound in the United States

10 9 8 7 6 5 4 3 2 1

Photos and Cover Design by North Cove Press
Yoga Poses (Asanas) by Lisa Sherman
Author's website
www.yogawithlisa.org

Dedication

I dedicate this book to my husband, Bob, and my daughter Catherine. Without both Bob and Catherine's support, patience, and sacrifice, I would not have been able to complete the 200-hour yoga teacher course. Without Bob's encouragement, support, and hours of editing and formatting this book would not have been completed. They help me to be my best self.

With Special Thanks to the yoga teachers who have helped me on my journey so far, especially, Alison (Ally) Goldenberg, Ashley Rose-Mello, and Susie Masters.

Thank you also, Gail Epstein for reading this work and giving amazing feedback to get the project completed.

Table of Contents

Introduction

What is Yoga?   1

Gifts I Have Received   5

Feel the Fear   11

Sun Salutation   13

Children's Yoga   17

The Eight Limbs Path   25

Finding Balance   27

Preparing a Yoga Lesson   33

Living in the Moment   37

Restorative Yoga   41

Philosophy   45

Anusara Yoga and Chakra Workshop   47

The First Written Test   49

Sound Healing   53

My First Two Hours of Teaching   59

Compassion   63

My Third Hour of Teaching   69

Sanskrit and Revolved Poses   71

Sequencing, Assists, and Inversions   75

Ripples in the Pond   79

The Gunas, Revolved Poses, More Inversions   83

Our Thirteenth Friday Class   85

My Fourth Hour of Teaching   89

Seated Poses and Yoga Nidra   91

Twists, Back Care and Back Bends   97

The Business of Yoga & Learning Contentment   99

Yoga Instruction at the Community Center   103

My Practicum Lesson   105

Anatomy with Chanel Luck   111

Family   113

Yoga Instruction Going Solo   115

Panic During Yoga   121

Kundalini Yoga   125

Ayurveda   127

Journey's End or Beginning?   129

Fast Forward Four Years   133

Lessons I Have Learned   135

Elementary Teacher Resources   139

Choosing a Studio   143

Coming to Terms   145

Introduction

Four years ago, at the age of 45, while working full time as an elementary teacher and caring for my family, I completed a 200-Hour Yoga Instructor's Program in the evenings and on weekends at the State of Grace Yoga and Wellness Center in Uxbridge, Massachusetts. I was lucky; I had the full support of my family, and the course was led by Susie Masters and Ashley Rose-Mello, who turned out be two of the most knowledgeable, experienced and all-around amazing women I have ever met.

While taking this course and practicing yoga at home, I blogged about my experiences, fears, growth and insights I gained on my website: www.yogawithlisa.org.

During this past year, (2017-2018) I have reread my posts and reflected on what I have learned since then and added those reflections under the heading "Fast Forward Four Years."

If you have ever wondered what it would be like to take a 200-hour yoga instructor's course, or if you ever wondered how such a course could benefit you, this book addresses those questions. You don't have to give up your career or become a yoga instructor to take this course. I am still a full-time elementary education teacher with a family at home. (Well, sort of: our daughter is now away at college.)

If you want to understand and practice yoga as it was historically meant to be, the 200-hour course with the right instructor will guide your journey down a path to good health, insight, and a measure of enlightenment that will change your life for the better, as it has changed mine.

What is Yoga?

The word *yoga* comes from the Sanskrit word "yuj", which means "to unite" or "to yoke". It is an ancient practice whose purpose is to unite an individual with his or her own true nature or higher self. According to yoga philosophy, everyone has a perfect self that can be reached if they free themselves from their egos and thoughts that cause their suffering.

The practice of yoga, as far as we know, began in northern India more than 5,000 years ago, before the availability of written records, well before the beginning of religions we practice today and long before the Greek culture that became the cradle of Western civilization.

Following those early periods, the practice of yoga changed with the times and the needs of the culture. The first systematic presentation of yoga, *The Eight Limbs Path*, was developed and written in the second century. That practice is considered classical yoga today.

During the long history of yoga, at least 40 branches have been developed. Two of those branches, Karma Yoga, which follows a path of service, and Jnana Yoga, which involves chanting and academic studies do not necessarily include the yoga poses we associate with the yoga we think of today, can also lead us to uniting ourselves with our "perfect selves" contained within.

THE
BHAGAVAD
GITA

A Walkthrough
for Westerners

JACK HAWLEY

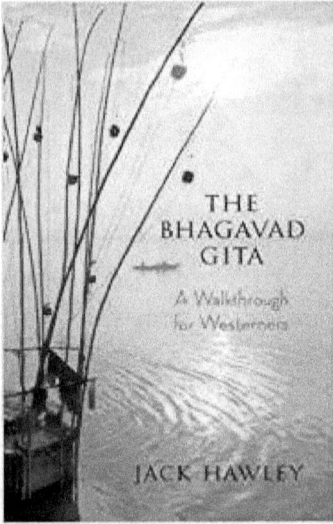

For an in-depth understanding of yoga's purpose and origins, read the *Bhagavad-Gîtâ* (Song of the Lord), a book written around 500 BCE that teaches the sacrifice of ego through self-knowledge. There are several versions of this book available in book stores and online.

In the late 1800s and early 1900s, yoga masters traveled to the United States lecturing on the universality of the world's religions. At the same time back in India, the Divine Life Society and other schools developed the practice of Hatha Yoga, which was later imported to the US, with a studio opening in Hollywood in 1947.

Hatha Yoga involves strengthening the body with postures, **asanas**, breath control for focusing, **pranayama** and **meditation**. From this, many teachers have attached their own ideas about postures, sequences, breathing exercises and other spiritual practices.

During the 20th century, the three main types of Hatha Yoga that came west were Iyengar, Ashtanga and Viniyoga. Over the years, different teachers developed additional branches of yoga from these.

An Iyengar practice is focused on careful alignment. Blocks, blankets and straps become an extension of the body and help with proper alignment. Ashtanga is the original Vinyasa (flow) yoga and is a more forceful style of yoga. Vinyasa or flow describes practices where poses transition smoothly from one to another. Movements are also synchronized with the breath. Viniyoga is more attentive, kind, and restorative. From these, many teachers have branched off further, and you can find

2

classes today within these traditions. For example, Ansura Yoga was influenced by Iyengar Yoga. Styles of yoga influenced by Ashtanga include Bikram (a form of hot yoga), Vinyasa, and Ana Forrest Yoga. Kundalini and Anusara are more spiritual practices, while Yin Yoga focuses on stretching connective tissue (as opposed to muscle) through careful alignment, as participants hold poses for longer periods.

In addition, you can find yoga classes for different purposes and populations, such as Children's Yoga, Prenatal Yoga, and Chair Yoga for the elderly or disabled. Mindfulness is currently one popular catchphrase heard in the West today to represent the yoga philosophy of living in the moment.

I believe that you can practice yoga poses by themselves to your heart's content, but without the breathing exercises, some form of meditative practice, and personal study, you will not get the full benefit of practicing yoga.

So, what is yoga? It's complicated.

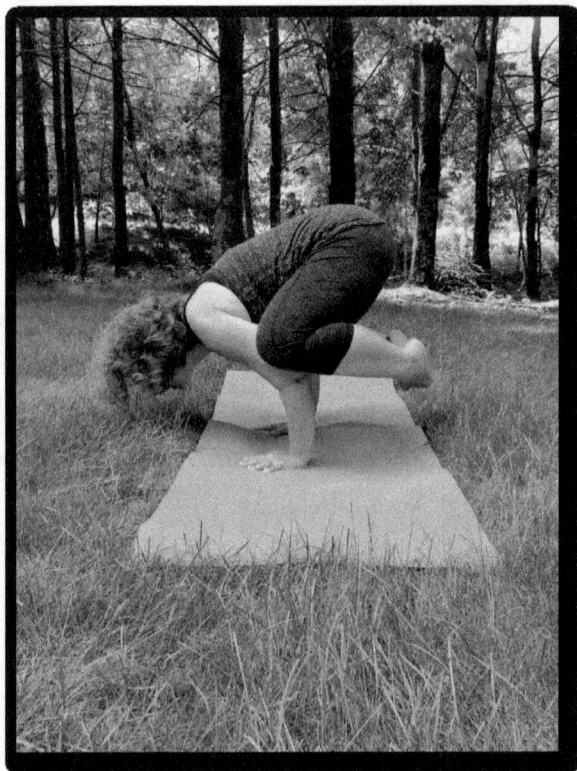

It's not easy, but someone has to do it it

Gifts I Have Received

First Website Entry 10/18/2013

Hi, I'm Lisa and I am writing to share my experience with you as I go through a 200-hour yoga teacher training course. I work during the day as a second-grade teacher and I have a family that needs my attention. Did I mention that I am also 45-years old and one of the older students in the class? I am set in my ways and my life is full of obligations, but I felt that I needed to try this and do more to enrich my life. This will be an adventure and I hope sharing my journey may encourage, inspire, or help someone else in some way.

Our journey has begun; at least that is what we were told by Susie Masters, one of the yoga teachers for the yoga instructor's course. Although I did not know it at the time, my journey began over three years ago when, on a whim, I walked into a free yoga class to "check it out". There I met the teacher, Alison (Ally) Goldenberg, who become my mentor.

I kept coming back to her class and I took other classes as well. I began learning about yoga and about my body - how it was working and how it *could* work. As I learned what it felt like to let go of anxiety caused by perceptions that were only real to me, like imagining ways someone might react or wondering what might happen if I did A or B, little by little I began to change. It probably was not enough for others to notice at first or maybe even now, but gradually I began to feel more whole. Encouraged, I began to research yoga, its history, mind-body connections, meditation and even Buddhism. I began to let go of things that made me miserable and live more fully in the present. I feel healthy and strong, despite recurrent knee problems. My arthritis, which bothered me constantly, is now under control, and the anxiety and migraines that were debilitating at times, are also under control. I no longer need to take medication for those issues. The gifts I received during those Sunday morning yoga classes have led me to taking this 200-hour instructor course, for the sole purpose of deepening my practice. Thank you, Alley, and God Bless.

My First Friday Class
10/18/2013

As I arrived at the beautiful old mill building, which housed my yoga studio, State of Grace (in Uxbridge, MA), I slowly walked up the brick walk and worked my way past the front desk into the familiar and comforting space with hard wood floors, soft lighting, and warm, light blue walls. I sat in a large circle already forming by other participants. When everyone arrived, there were around 22 participants of diverse ages. There was one man, and the rest were women. As we introduced ourselves, I discovered a group of people with a variety of backgrounds, professions, and people at all different stages of life. They came from Massachusetts, Rhode Island, and even New Hampshire. We were all taking the class with differing goals in mind. What we did have in common, though, was that everyone was there to learn, grow, and enrich their lives. I'm looking forward to growing with this group of people.

I am a "wee bit" terrified that I will be less available to my family, friends, and work as I take the time to complete this course. I am also a little bit scared that I won't be good at it, but what I've learned so far is that if you take one step at a time and deal with one day and one moment at a time, you can do amazing things. By eliminating the worry about the past and the future you are able to do more and to live more fully in the moment. This week I need to do some reading on the history of yoga, and I've got to collect my husband or daughter to let me practice "teaching" them the sun salutation, since that is my assignment for class next Friday.

Second Friday Class
10/25/2013

Six hours down (194 to go). Tonight, the class practiced teaching. We taught a partner the Sun Salutation sequence and then we taught two different people to do two of the poses from the Sun Salutation in greater detail. We were all petrified. Our bodies knew how to do the individual poses, but it was difficult to find the words to describe to our classmates what they needed to do with each pose. We stumbled through, however, and we felt more comfortable, if not competent, each time we went through the process. The comforting part was that we all seemed to feel the same way; even those of us who were already teachers in another setting. One participant thought it would be a lot easier for those of us who were teachers, but yoga was a new subject and we were all starting at the same level.

This week, a couple of us decided to talk ourselves through some poses out loud to gain more awareness and practice. Susie, our instructor from Scotland, reminded us not to take away from our personal practice time, which is easy to do when you have to spend so much time learning the lessons for the next class. She explained that you can't give more than you have, and that you need your own practice to grow and increase what you are able to give.

Susie would say: "Be a teacher when you are a teacher but be a student when you are a student."

Fast Forward Four Years

I found the idea of separating out the role of being a student of yoga and a teacher of yoga to be very valuable for me when I began teaching some sessions at my elementary school. When I practiced for the lessons for the classes I was going to teach, it didn't have the same calming effect on me as when I practiced yoga for myself. As teachers we are thinking about the needs of our students, their safety, and what we will share. As students who are also continuing to practice yoga for ourselves, we are listening to our bodies and minds and responding to those needs.

When I started teaching, I needed so much practice to prepare for a class that it was hard to take time to practice for myself. As I became more experienced, though, I needed less time to feel confident and to remember the sequences, and I was able to find more balance. I did need to practice yoga just for me. Sometimes I did this separately, but I also found that when I practiced the sequence I was going to teach, I could add poses and look inward between planned sequence poses to meet my own needs and then focus back onto the class sequence.

For example, if my class sequence was to move from Warrior I to Humble Warrior to Warrior II, I may pause between Humble Warrior and Warrior II, focus on my breath, and add a balance pose (like Warrior III) for refocusing just for me. I knew I wasn't going to be doing that with my beginners when I taught the class, but I was able to refocus myself and look inward for a moment.

I practice yoga at home a few times a week and once a week at my studio class. While these sessions are for me, I may take note of an aspect of the class or a sequence I may want to use either in my classes or at home in my daily practice, but I always try to focus back on my breath and my current needs to gain the peaceful feeling, which was the original purpose for attending a yoga class.

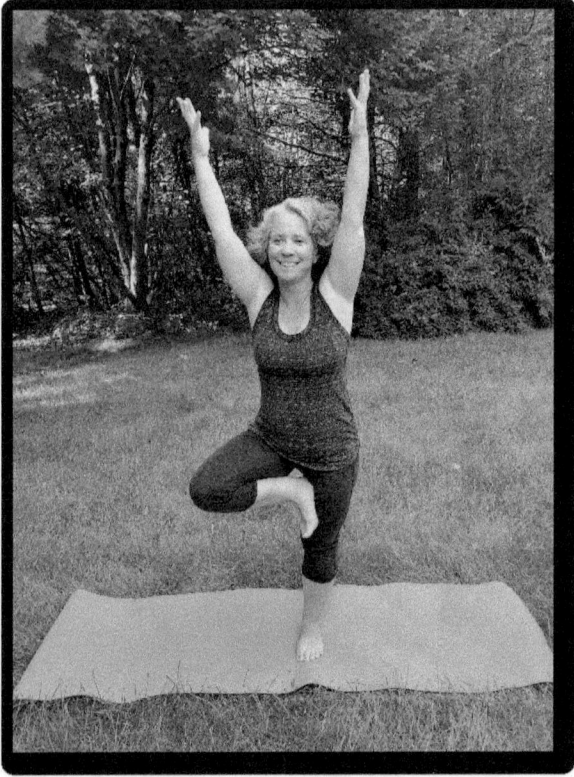

Vrksasana   Tree Pose

Feel the Fear

First Weekend
10/25-27/2013

My first "yoga weekend" included 15 hours of teacher training plus my Sunday morning weekly class. That added up to 19 hours at my yoga studio plus driving time. With fifteen hours of learning and being exposed to new or forgotten material, it's no wonder I feel overwhelmed! When I arrived at my Sunday yoga class (after our first Saturday class was complete), I found that many people were feeling the same way. Others who arrived were talking to the teacher and telling her how overwhelmed they were by the weekend - even before the class began. Knowing that others felt the same way at the same moment didn't change the amount of work that had to be done, but it did make me feel better about my own feelings. Given the universal experience, it took some of the pressure off.

We learned about anatomy, structural supports, seasonal yoga, and breathing. We performed and taught each other how to progress through the Sun Salutation (or at least we tried to give clear instructions to each other, which was harder than it seemed), and we broke down many poses and experimented with assists. This was all on Friday and Saturday. We haven't even started the last six hours of the weekend! My head is spinning, and I look forward to the next couple of days to slow down enough to process it all.

"Feel the fear but do it anyway." That is how Susie started the class today. I'll try to keep that in mind. Interestingly, I felt a lot less fear today, but when I realized that my next 15-hour weekend was coming up fast, the fear returned. I'm just starting to get caught up at work after the last 15-hour weekend. I feel like I haven't seen my family for over a week and I haven't been able to do my usual household chores, which, requiring little thought, can calm me down and rest my nerves. Next weekend is a long weekend, thankfully, so I will have one less day of work the following week. My parent-teacher conferences for school are over, and other personal stressors of the previous week have passed, so it should be OK, but I am afraid I have overextended myself. I hope I can do this. I hope I can do the extra homework in addition to my normal workload. I hope I can learn to do this well. I need to work on speaking louder and giving clearer directions. I also need to learn the Sanskrit names of many poses that I don't know that well. I guess what I'm really describing is fear. I won't know how it will go until I try. I guess I need to "Feel the fear and do it anyway".

Sun Salutation

Friday Class
11/1/2013

As I talked with my husband about teaching the Sun Salutation (described in more detail later in the chapter: "Preparing a Yoga Lesson", Flash Forward Four Years"), I was thinking out loud about how to explain it, what the pace should be, and what prompts to use when he asked me a key question: "Toward which populations are the directions directed?" I stopped for a moment because it finally dawned on me that the directions aren't supposed to be directed at any *type* of population in-as-much as they should be directed at the students in front of us at the time. It is so obvious that, being a teacher, it should have hit me right away.

If there is a beginner in front of you, obviously they will not be able to do the Sun Salutation as a flow without a lot of breakdown of the poses, modeling and slow work on each step. That is how I will need to teach my husband and anyone else who volunteers, if they have little or no experience. If I do a class with my daughter and her friends who have some yoga experience, I could get away with less instruction for each pose relying on cues and prompts to achieve proper alignment and engagement of all muscles. I have to teach like I do at school with my second graders; that is, according to their needs at the time.

Teaching yoga requires a lot of practice, but I know that practice will pay off. I do feel better today about next weekend being another "yoga weekend". Something I've learned over the last several years of yoga is that feelings are like the weather in New England—if you don't like them, just wait a minute and they will change. In other words, if you obsess over your feelings and don't let the go, and if you think of all the possible outcomes based on your worry, you will make yourself miserable. On the other hand, if you let yourself experience these feelings without obsessing over them, and if you trust that whatever happens next you will handle even if you don't predict it ahead of time, then the feeling will pass and be replaced by a different emotion. It really works. It is part of being in the present and experiencing what is happening now and in real time.

When you think about all the possible scenarios for things that could go wrong and plan for every possibility, you are not spending time in the present. You are not in reality. You are lost in what ifs that may never happen and, even if they do happen, are you really able to cope better because you had nightmares about them last week? You also lose the simple joys of the moment—such as the feeling you get from the warm water in the sink as you wash the dishes, the hurried hug you get from your teenager as she runs out the door to her next activity, the view of the graceful and majestic deer eating your neighbor's plants and shrubs even when you know yours will be next.

My concern as to whether I could teach a yoga pose passed and many other stressors of the last week are gone. This coming week is a new week; I can do it and I will do my best, which is all we can ask of ourselves. It will be worth the work when I reach the end of the training.

Last night and today I tried to let go of feelings I didn't need (fear and anxiety) to make room for the more important positive attitude and faith. Just as you point your eyes where you want to go when you are skiing downhill, you can point your mind to where you want to be, in the ditch or skimming smoothly over fresh powder snow.

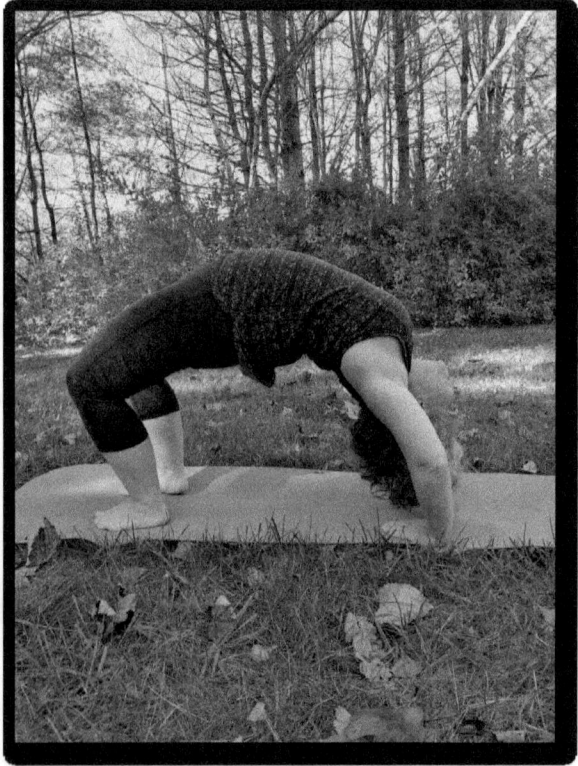

Urdhva Dhanurasana
Upward Bow (Wheel) Pose

Children's Yoga

Weekend
11/8-10/2013

We finished our Friday session after having spent a lot of time learning and teaching several standing poses. I found the poses that I spent the week going through went much smoother in my teaching than the ones we looked at and learned Friday night. Makes sense, right? Therefore, what I need to do is break down poses, write out possible cues and study the step-by-step breakdown of the poses, and then I will be able to figure out what cues to give for different alignment issues. I was able to help my first partner much more with that kind of preparation.

If you are thinking about taking a teacher training course, I recommend that as you practice yoga for yourself, you take some time to think about how your body gets into the poses, how each pose feels, and where you need to work on the integrity of the poses. I don't mean that you should do that all the time, because you do need your practice (remember student vs. teacher mind), but at some point, you should think about the poses in a sequential step-by-step manner.

Saturday
11/9/2013

Our class spent this morning with Ashley Rose-Mello learning about children's yoga. I thought that would really resonate with me since I am an elementary teacher. Ashley was incredible; if I had a young child of my own, I would bring him or her to Ashley's class every day. She was enthusiastic and fun. You could tell she loved teaching children's yoga. In the same way, I like the idea of teaching children with disabilities, as that is my first true love in teaching. Even though I love teaching second graders, I always fall in love with the children who have special needs. I find they always have something to teach me through their unique way of viewing the world. No matter how enthusiastic, however, right now children's yoga seems too much like what I already do all day at work. Yoga is my place for restoring my energy and regrouping so that I have more to offer to my little ones at school. I'm not sure I could go from school to a children's yoga class and still do my best; at least not at this moment.

Ashley did recommend some things I would like to check out, such as "Brain Gym", which I can incorporate into my class routines. I already have my students move in between sitting activities (we call it "getting the wiggles out") and the children love it. I can now add in some across-the-midline activities and whatever else I might find when I research it. Maybe I can share some of the research with parents and other teachers in my school.

One thing Ashley did say about children's yoga was to: "Let go of the expectation that it will be a perfect class." She was referring to the fact that children's classes can be noisy, chaotic, and unpredictable. I think what she said can apply to any class we teach, as well as to life. If you can let go of the expectations and your attachment to a certain outcome, then you can better appreciate, experience and enjoy your instruction time.

We are halfway through our Saturday session and at this moment we are about to resolve or at least consider the question, "What is Yoga?" We are also planning to look at the Eight Limbs Path of yoga. Are we ready? Of course we are! There has been so much information and, more importantly, so many new things to learn on my own.

During the second half of our day with Susie we went through the beginnings of western yoga. We drew the tree of yoga, with its different branches and its roots coming from India. We learned a little bit of history (and we still have a lot more to learn; it is impossible to cover 5,000 years in a couple of hours). We learned about the many different branches of yoga—the types of teachings that have spread and the diverse ways in which people experience and live the Eight Limbs Path. (See next chapter for a brief description.) We spent the most time on the teachings of Sri Krishnamacharya who's teaching greatly influenced yoga in the west. His work and the work of others can be seen in most styles of teaching in the United States today. There is more research that I want to do, and I was drawn to one style. Susie recommended a couple of books which I plan to check out.

Discussing the Eight Limbs Path was fascinating and brought me back to the classes I had with Ally. She incorporated the ideas into her classes. At that time, it all seemed very foreign, yet soothing and thought-provoking at the same time. The last year that Ally taught at the first studio where we met, was a particularly hard for me. My mother was diagnosed with lung cancer and suffered greatly for four months as we tried to be there for her, to comfort her and my father, and to help her through the ordeal. Right before my mother passed away, Ally was going to be leaving the studio. At the last class she taught she brought me the book, "Meditations from the Mat", by Rolf Gates, with whom Ally had recently trained. She gave me her copy as she felt that it would be of help to me. I will always remember her thoughtfulness, care, and kindness. This, for me, was what the Yamas of the Eight Limbs Path could look like in real life.

The book also made the Eight Limbs even clearer. Rolf Gates came from a background I could relate to, and he spoke in language that was accessible to anyone, even if you knew nothing about the Eight Limbs Path. His book is set up in short daily devotions with quotes and words of wisdom from an amazing variety of sources to show how to interpret each of the components of the teachings. He never claimed to have all of the answers and he chose people from all walks of life to draw wisdom from. The book and teachings have taught me a lot and sent me in directions for my own learning that I would have never predicted; taking this 200-hour teacher training course, for example.

Sunday
11/10/13

Wow!! Amazing!! That is what comes to mind after our Sunday session with Nadja, a Certified Iyengar Yoga Teacher. Nadja was just lovely; that is the best way to describe her. She is tall and lean with a dancer's body and she has a beautiful smile that lit up the room. The smile had a bit of the devil in it at times (like when she suggested hot Epsom salt baths for all of us tonight).

She knew she was pushing us, but she also knew how to motivate us to keep at it. Even when we were exhausted at the end of the night, many of us were still trying to jump out of the poses like she taught us, even though crawling out of the poses seemed more doable. She glowed from the inside and, even though she worked us hard with over four hours of asanas in one day, she kept us motivated and eager to learn as much as we could. The Iyengar yoga was different from what I was used to, although I could see the influence in Susie's classes. Some of the cues and ways in and out of poses taught by Susie were similar to some of the approaches Nadja took with us. It was definitely not a flow class. Nadja demonstrated the poses, we tried them, she corrected us and demonstrated them again, and we tried them again and again. She was tough, but she was helpful, kind, and respectful. Her grace and patience with those of us who didn't demonstrate her perfect form was something I hope to emulate in my own yoga teaching.

Nadja's goal was to help us get to the next level in our own time and she stressed listening to our bodies. She was constantly asking how we felt in each posture, watching for possible stresses on the body, and finding ways to modify each pose so we could reap the benefit from the action and come a little closer to the conventional pose. She called it "action", as opposed to movement; the difference being that action is purposeful, unlike movement. It was an incredible experience. I don't necessarily feel drawn to Iyengar yoga at this time although the rules and specific requirements are appealing to me, but I learned so much from this experience. I would definitely be open to taking some Iyengar classes later and I would be very interested in trying another workshop with Nadja if the opportunity presented itself. I am very grateful for the opportunity to have had this training and I am grateful to my teachers for bringing her into our class.

Flash Forward Four Years

When I started my yoga teacher training, I did not see myself teaching a children's yoga class. I had too much to learn about yoga and about which elements are crucial to feel confident sharing what I loved about yoga with children. I know children very well and the idea of trying to slow them down and have them follow directions seemed impossible, but what I've learned since my teacher training is that isn't the most important part of the process.

The key ingredient is teaching children to breathe, move their bodies, and be more aware of how breaths and movements affect their bodies and minds. To do this, games, animal sounds (for example meowing and hissing for happy/sad cat, or blowing raspberries while doing camel pose), stories, or partner activities may be more appropriate for bringing children to the moment. As you plan activities or sequences, ask yourself, "Are there more developmentally appropriate and engaging ways of teaching this idea or action?" Incorporating the question, "How does this movement, string of movements, or type of breath make your body feel?" into your children's class or activity helps them learn about themselves.

I started very slowly by adding breaths and motions to my second-grade classroom as part of a morning meeting or for classroom breaks. We talked about how these made the students feel, and we also learned that feelings are fleeting and that everyone is different, so each person must listen to his or her own body. I've encouraged children to regularly verbalize things they are grateful for, as well as, qualities they like about themselves and others. This year I've also started teaching my second graders positive affirmations to increase positive thoughts.

As I saw the benefits in my class, I ran training for other teachers in my building with regard to what I was doing. When I saw some interest at my school, I went to a day workshop with Lisa Flynn, E-RYT, RCYT (of ChildLight Yoga) about mindfulness activities and yoga for classrooms, and I have been reading Lisa Flynn's book "Yoga for Children". I recommend both the training and the book. After that, I tried looking online for more information. I expect to continue looking for opportunities to learn, but I also plan to begin looking for the right time and opportunities to teach children in the future at my school, the library, or the local YMCA. My advice in this instance is to understand that you and your circumstances are always changing and to be open to these new perspectives, experience, feelings, and understandings. Allow yourself to change and grow.

I love the line from Lewis Carroll's book Alice *in Wonderland* that says, "I can't go back to yesterday, because I was a different person then."

I have developed and published some yoga exercises for teachers to use with elementary aged children in the classroom. These are free and can be downloaded from my website: www.yogawith lisa.org. From the menu bar click on "Teacher Resources".

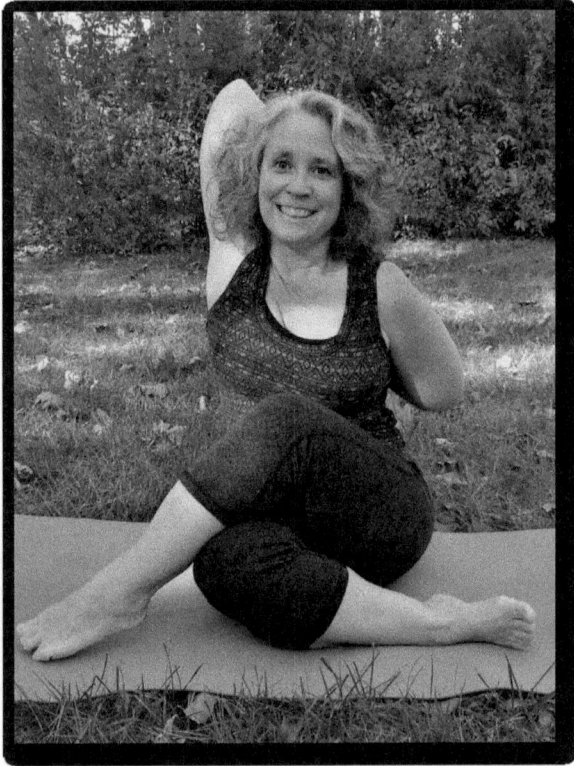

Gomukhasana   Cow Face Pose

The Eight Limbs Path

Here I hope to give you a brief understanding of Patanjali's Eight Limbs Path of Yoga. Keep in mind these limbs are often shown in a circle. They are not necessarily sequential. You can jump in and out of the circle in any order according to your current interests, needs, and opportunities. For example, I started with Asanas and then began studying the Yamas, and other limbs.

The first limb described includes the *Yamas,* or The Five Moral Restraints. These are basically related to how we treat ourselves and others in the world around us. Included are *Ahimsa* (non-violence), *Satya* (truthfulness), *Asteya* (non-stealing), *Brahmacarya* (moderation) and *Aparigraha* (non-hoarding). These are characteristics we may try to incorporate into our lives and they can be interpreted in more than the above ways. *Ahimsa,* for example, is often interpreted more broadly as kindness to self and others or as non-harming, as opposed to just non-violent. The idea is that trying to bring these values into our lives will increase the good we bring to the world and help us to move along the path toward enlightenment.

Next come the Niyamas, or *The Five Observances.* These include *Sauca* (purity), *Santosa* (contentment), *Tapas* (austerity), *Svadhyaya* (self-study) and *Isvara-pranidhana* (devotion to a higher power). The next limb includes *Asanas,* which are the poses more commonly associated with yoga. A yoga teacher may focus a class on any of the limbs or aspects of the limbs, but many people think of the poses only when they think about "doing yoga".

Pranayama, another limb, is connected to breathing consciously and mindfully. When a teacher talks about focusing on the breath or teaches a specific type of breathing that elicits different body responses, like three-part breath, ujjayi breath, nadi shodhana, etc., Pranayama is the focus. Breathing exercises are used in a traditional yoga asana class as well as during meditation. Connecting movement to breath is a big part of some yoga traditions as it slows the breath, extends the inhale and/or the exhale and, in some cases, it can include breath retention. The way we breathe has major impacts in the way our minds and bodies respond to our environment. It can calm our minds and bodies, or it can send us into a fight or flight response.

The next two limbs are, in my mind, beginning to move more toward mindfulness and more spiritual practices. These are *Pratyahara* (turning inward) and *Dharan*a (concentration).

Dhyana (meditation) is another limb. It leads to the Eighth Limb of *Samadhi* which, according to Rolf Gates and Katrina Kenison in *Meditations from the Mat*, is the *Union of the Self with Object of Meditation*. Others call it Enlightenment. There are many sources for learning more about the Eight Limbs Path, but Rolf Gates' book, *Meditations from the Mat*, is one of my favorites because he writes a daily lesson that includes quotes and life stories to show how each of these limbs fit into our real lives. The author acknowledges that we are human and therefore don't always have a smooth path in life. Of course, some bumps are of our own making, but again, that is our human state. Despite this we can interpret the *Eight Limbs Path* and make the values part of our lives and the world better.

Finding Balance

Friday
11/15/2013

I have yet to find balance in my current activities—work, home, and family responsibilities. I have struggled with a presumption that I must meet everyone's needs or expectations perfectly. The study of yoga has helped a lot over the last few years, but every year work becomes more demanding and I struggle to cut non-essential work and accept that I can't do everything that I believe is expected of me.

Right now, I spend between eight and ten hours at work Monday through Friday, and often bring work home. At home I do housework, make supper, and try to spend quality time with my family. I've now added a yoga course that I think will bring amazing benefits in the long run as I learn and grow, but to get these benefits, I have to put some time and effort into the practice and study of yoga, which will add to an already overcrowded schedule.

I have to figure out how to reduce my public-school teaching work load, and learn how to leave my work problems at school. That is a process I'm getting better at, but I have a way to go.

If we only had to teach our students, life would be wonderful, but that is not the case. Administrative and clerical paperwork, which has grown to impracticable levels require hours of time on the computer at home. Classroom and teacher-prep time interruptions also increase the workload at home and cheat my students out of their learning time. I've been trying to figure out how to stem the tide.

I have one period free of children and I usually spend two to three hours after school preparing for the next day to adequately address each student's individual developmental level, knowledge background and skill level in each subject that I teach. I also try to catch up on the weekends with work that is left over. What I have realized is that meetings with coworkers who come in my room to work with students in my class and co-teach take up a big part of my time. I have to make sure the cost/benefit for the time spent is worth the time and worth losing the feeling of balance and having the eventual feeling that all my energy is gone. (Ahimsa and Satya?)

I'm doing my best to do all the work the school department asks, but not at my expense or my family's. I have been working on it, but I tend to always say yes when asked, "Do you have a minute?" I need to start being truthful and say, "I really don't.", "I can't until I finish.", or "Maybe I will be free later." I have been starting to say that to friends who plan with me after school, but I feel like I'm letting them down. I've got to remember that my family's time and welfare is of much greater importance than the committee work after school. I've got to let go of the guilt. I'm getting better at that, but I've got to improve even more.

I also have to be honest enough to tell anyone who asks why something is not done that there was no time left in the day. I am doing myself harm (*Ahisma*) by not controlling what I spend my time on. I am also stealing from my family time (*Asteya*) by not making wiser choices and being honest with others that think they need my time (Satya). Even though I have studied the Yamas before, it is essential to revisit them regularly and continue to put the effort forth to live them and to learn more about how they apply to my life.

I resigned my position as Teacher Leader in the spring last year. I admitted that someone else could pick up that particular job and, even though it meant a pay decrease, it was a good decision.

Not all extra work and meetings are equally important or of value to the education of my children. I tend to be obsessive and I try to do everything well, but I need to learn to prioritize and let things go that don't get done recognizing that everything is not of equal value to my children.

When I sat down to write this I was feeling very unbalanced, sad, and undirected as to what I should do. Now I feel better. Even though the things I've been thinking about are hard for me to face and fix because of my desire to do everything well and not disappoint, I think I realized that I have taken steps to start helping myself take control, which means I can continue to take further steps. Even one step towards something good leads to another.

Fast Forward Four Years

So where am I four years later? Life is still a balancing act; that won't change because my life is full. Looking back, I'm not sure how I did everything, but I did accomplish what I set out to do. Part of the stress over the workload was looking outward to assess my self-worth, which I had believed was tied to how others viewed me or to whether I met everyone else's expectations. Silly me. To be successful with all the pressure, I had to really think about priorities. I had to learn to do less at work - a lesson I am still working on but beginning to master. I had to let go of other people's expectations of me and focus on my own priorities and needs. What was most important to me? How do I want to spend my time? What will I remember as I grow older and what do I want others to remember about me? I had to say "no" at times when others made plans for my time, especially related to work. Again, I am doing that more naturally now.

The two things at the top of my list are taking time to care of myself and my family. I do work hard for my children at school, but I know the things that impact my students are a higher priority than requests to meet the administrative needs of the district. Things that won't make me a better teacher for my students drop down on my priority list. To fit it all in, I analyze the to-do list, focus on what is most important for my students, and let go of the distractions.

I've learned to do what I can and not worry about what is left over. I also remember that everyone is a being of light with value and goodness inside. Our intrinsic value isn't dependent on what we do or on others' views of us. Tasks will fill the full amount of time available. The theme that I follow, and the one I recommend to others, is to be clear about your priorities, accept your limits, and free yourself from the expectations of others.

Saturday
11-16-23

Last night each of us taught a pose (not of our own choice) to a small group that included half of our class, about 10 people.

I didn't feel as frightened as I expected. I did stumble over the directions, but I think I did as well as some of my classmates. We all have different strengths and talents and we are learning a lot from each other. Some have soothing voices, others have good timing, give clear directions, etc. Eventually we'll all get better and our weaknesses will become our strengths. We can see aspects we like in each other's teaching, which gives us more to aspire to.

Last night it felt good to have Susie complement my mirroring of *Virabhadrasana* II. Mirroring is the teacher showing the pose in front of the students, which is the same as students looking in a mirror when looking at the teacher. This works as long as the teacher remembers that her left side is their right side. I never even thought about the mirroring as I was struggling with the steps and verbiage, and it was interesting and exciting to think that I could do that part, at least for one pose at a time, without thinking about it. Most of the teachers I have had mirrored as they taught, so I guess I learned from watching. I think if I can stay relaxed, I will do much better.

I volunteered to teach the Sun Salutation with three standing poses to the entire class next Friday. Today I wrote out pages of directions to the sequence and I practiced on my daughter. She has an injured foot, so she couldn't do most of it, but she listened to some of the directions. When I asked her how I did, she said that I needed to sound more confident and speak louder. I then asked if I was at least better than the last time I tried it with her, but she said that I did better last time, probably because of my cold, which is softening my voice even more than usual. She is a tough critic, but she is truthful and calls things the way she sees them. I'm glad that she has learned to do that. I'll keep practicing, I'll try to be confident, and I'll hope for the best. I have to remember what Susie said. If you make a mistake, you learn from it and will do better next time. My hope is that I'll get more comfortable in front of the group, using the language, and going through the poses every time I do it. Our group is so supportive and encouraging of each other. We are very lucky.

Fast Forward Four Years

Comfort while teaching does come. After I completed this course, I volunteered to teach community yoga classes with some of my classmates who went on to put together a yoga collaborative to give the community the opportunity to experience yoga. I also taught a few classes at a public library and I have run many sessions of classes at my work. As you practice, the confidence comes. The anxiety when you do make a mistake is reduced (and you do make fewer mistakes). With every class, with every success, and with every error, you learn and grow. It does get easier.

Preparing a Yoga Lesson

Thursday
11/21/2013

This past week, I prepared to teach my class the *Surya Namaskar* A (Sun Salutation A) in addition to three standing poses. I was very nervous about teaching the whole class, but now that I've done it, I think it will be easier next time. Here's what I did to prepare. First, I looked at the transitions in *Surya Namaskar* A and positions that might flow easily to the extra standing poses. I decided to have the class move from the upward salute to a chair pose (Utkatasana). I then decided to add Warrior I and III (Virabhadrasana I and III) after the first runners lunge. I later found out that this was very similar to *Surya Namaskar* B (Sun Salutation B), which we will be learning soon in class. After choosing the extra poses I looked up each pose and reviewed my texts.

I then wrote out the sequence, including how to describe each pose and describe how to perform it, which muscles to engage and how to align the body in each pose. I read it through each night and practiced going through the verbal litany in my head and aloud. As I felt more comfortable following that process, I tried it out loud by myself. It was hard this past week to find a volunteer to follow my instructions, but I think that would have added to my confidence. As the week progressed, I decided to

My Yoga Journey   Lisa Sherman

have the students focus on being present and focus on how their bodies felt as they did each pose. Learning to be present is one part of yoga that has made an incredible difference in my life, so it is going to be part of any yoga I share or teach. By the end of the week I felt that I was prepared to teach the sequence Friday night. I was focused on doing well, and was not as anxious as I had expected to be. I reminded myself all week what Susie has been telling us: "If you make a mistake, you will learn from it and you will not make that same mistake again."

Fast Forward Four Years

The Sun Salutation, or Surya Namaskar A, is a sequence in yoga that can be used as a warm up, as a flow sequence by itself, as part of a full class sequence, or as a strengthening sequence. Surya Namaskar B has the same basic structure, with some variations from A. Each movement can be linked to either an inhale or an exhale. Generally upward and heart opening movements are done on an inhale, while downward and closed movements are done on an exhale.

As I learned it, Surya Namaskar A starts in Tadasana (Mountain Pose), moves to Pranamasana (Prayer Pose), then inhale to Urdhva Hastasana (Upward Salute), then you fold and exhale to Uttanasana (Forward Fold), come halfway up to Ardha Uttanasana (flat back) on the inhale, then fold again with the exhale. Next, inhale as you step back with one foot into a Anjaneyasana (Low Lunge), then exhale to Uttihita Chaturanga Dandasana (High Plank), to Chaturanga Dandasana (come to the floor), and inhale up to Urdhva Mukha Svanasana (Upward Facing Dog). After that, you exhale as you move to Adho Mukha Svanasana (Downward Facing Dog). And finally, you raise the leg you stepped back with first, then bring it back to the front of your mat, followed by your second leg. Repeat from the beginning, stepping back with the opposite leg.

This sequence engages every part of the body and can be a good introduction to flow. It can be meditative in the repetition and easy flow from one move to the next. You can also find many variations and modifications online, so it is accessible to most people. There are some variations to the Sun Salutation depending upon your instructor. Below is one example.

Sun Salutation design by: Nsanja Yaday

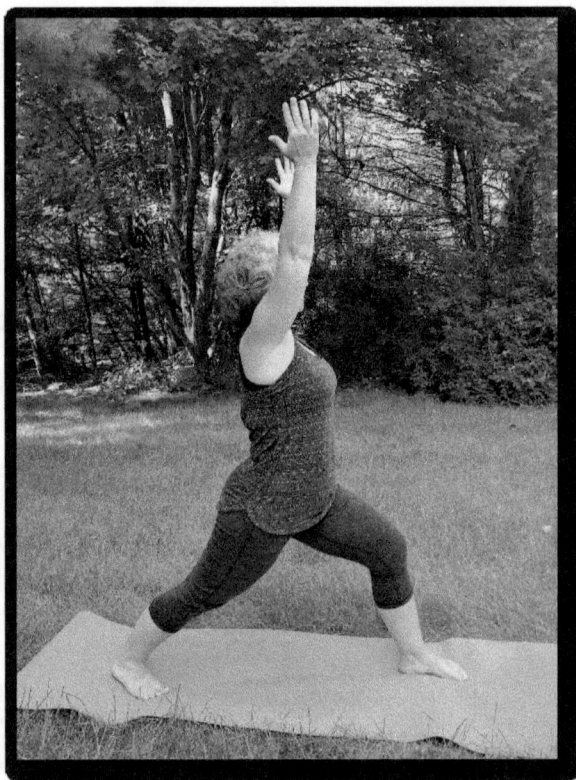

Virabhadrasana I Warrior I

36

Living in the Moment

Friday
11/22/2013

We had an amazing class tonight. First another student led us in a breathing activity and did a fantastic job. She really clarified "alternate nostril breathing" for us. Then I was able to teach my sequence (Sun Salutation A with three additional standing poses). I was a little less nervous than I expected and it went relatively well. I received some great feedback that helped build my confidence. I know I have a way to go to be ready to teach a regular full class, but I also know I'm taking steps toward that with each day of practice and each class. Another student taught her sequence and then we had a "clinic" to wrap up standing poses. In the clinic we took turns teaching individual standing poses to another classmate as everyone watched and called out things they noticed. We were able to learn a lot from each other and from our teachers because as we saw mistakes being made, we could find out from each other and our teachers how to correct them with words and assists.

When I taught my sequence, I asked students to be particularly mindful of their bodies and to stay focused on the moment. Because this has been life altering to me, it will be a theme I will use often in my teaching. I used to have frequent issues with anxiety and I could work myself up into a frenzy easily by replaying old conversations in my head and thinking about what I should have said or done. I could also spend tremendous amounts of time and energy thinking about what might happen and replaying possible scenarios and outcomes of possible events. I thought I was preparing myself for the future, but in reality, I was cheating myself out of living in real time. Events and thoughts that are past are not real anymore, nor are imagined events that have not happened yet. I was wasting the existing moment, living in the memory of a moment that was already gone by, or living in a future that was most unlikely to ever occur.

I was wasting my energy and time. This focus on the unreal caused a lot of discomfort, unease, anxiety and physical symptoms that were unnecessary. Life is challenging enough without causing our own pain based on things that are not real. I started learning about living in the moment and being present for asanas (postures in yoga). Then I began to learn to live in the moments outside of my asana classes.

I started realizing that if I were present in the moment, then I could handle whatever came up even if I hadn't thought it all out ahead of time. Let experiences, feelings and moments in, then let them pass through you and out, like fleeting clouds in the sky. If you can do that, you will be ready for the next moment and not miss it. I've started reading a book Susie recommended, "Living Your Yoga" by Judith Lasater, PH.D., P.T. In the first few pages she explains that, "We spend most of our time forgetting to feel, to sense, and to know life—moment by moment." I feel like my yoga practice has given back to me the ability to do that. That doesn't mean I do that all the time; I am human. It is a process, but the asanas, breathing, and changing my thought patterns to attempt to focus on the present moment have helped me to do a better job of living in the moment and letting go when the moment is over. Part of my desire to take this teaching course is to learn how to share this knowledge with someone else.

Fast Forward Four Years

I want to clarify that living in the moment does not mean you won't have uncomfortable feelings. We are human, and we all have uncomfortable experiences and feelings: sadness, anxiety, anger, etc. The key is that when something happens, and you feel these things, notice them, react to the situation as it is happening, and then let it pass. The important point is not to fuel negative feelings by:

1. Creating a narrative around the feeling by taking from past experiences, or 2. Creating a narrative of "what ifs" that brings you into an imaginary future.

With regard to the first, an example would be getting angry with something my boss does and spinning a tale in my head about every issue we have ever had and every complaint I have had about him or my work. In doing this, I would be fueling the anger that in turn would cloud my judgment, and I wouldn't be able to form an appropriate course of action in response to that single event. I would also be attaching myself to the anger and holding onto it so it couldn't pass away naturally and be gone.

I find now that I am able to discover what is bothering me quicker than in the past, which allows the accompanying emotion, anger for example, to rise to the surface rather than remain submerged eating away at me for long periods of time;

and then handle that emotion quickly and appropriately letting it go.

An example of the second way of losing the moment would be if I had a teenager who was late, and I became anxious, which is natural. There are many responses or reactions; obviously, how late my teen was would determine the appropriate course of action. The response may be to call where she was supposed to be, or it might be to wait and see (which is very hard to do). It is very uncomfortable waiting, but it is worse if you start thinking about every frightening hypothetical reason, she might be late. If I were to obsess about the possibility of an accident, for example, I would be increasing my uncomfortable feelings when it might be that the teenager merely lost track of time. I would be making myself more and more anxious, sad, angry, fearful, etc. when nothing has actually happened.

When I project myself into the future, which I rarely do during these situations now, I tell myself that no matter what happens I can handle it, or I tell myself to wait to see what does happen. With the normal stresses life has to offer, this has helped me immensely. It takes the pressure off, so I don't have to deal with feelings about something that I think might happen. By living in the moment, my emotions are connected to reality, not separate from it. I have found this to be a life changing approach to living that has dramatically improved the quality of my life.

Restorative Yoga

Friday
12/6/2013

I love the idea of restorative yoga, and Jessica, a teacher from my yoga studio came to teach us about this practice Friday night. She was very energetic, kind, and sincere. The class was great and the poses felt good. Many of the things she showed us I'd done in some way as part of my yoga classes through the years, but it was good to put them in a category and begin to group styles and types of practices.

Props were very important to this practice and I learned a great deal about how to use blankets, bolsters, sand bags, eye pillows, and straps to help someone get the benefits from poses even if they can't independently hold the given pose. I started thinking about ways to use materials around the house that might mimic some of the studio materials. The idea of restorative yoga is that someone can hold the pose longer with props, relax into the pose (which was wonderful), feel a little pampered, without strain, and gain the benefits of slow opening and stretching.

We didn't go through a full sequence, but we learned several poses and ways to support the body. I plan to find out more about this type of yoga and how to run a complete restorative class and how to incorporate some restorative work into a typical sequence. I plan to read more about this as I finish some of the other research I've been doing. With every class, I learn so much and realize that I have so much more to learn.

Savasana is not one of my strengths. I prefer a movement-based meditation. I can stay focused during asanas most of the time at this point because of the many body sensations to keep my mind in the moment, but I find breath work, meditation, and savasana more challenging as far as keeping my mind still and letting thoughts come in *and* out. I am getting better, but that is one part of my practice I'm still working on. Regarding that, though, I found the use of sandbags and eye pillows shown in this class grounding and helpful during savasana. At my yoga class (for my personal weekly practice), I used a sandbag across my lower abdomen, and because it drew attention to the breath in my belly, it made it easier to focus on the breath when I was still. I will try a sandbag on my forehead and eye pillows on my hands at some point as well, to see how they feel.

Ironically, in the middle of the night after the instructors' restorative yoga class, I woke up with significant pain in my back under my shoulder blade, which radiated toward the front of my chest around my clavicle. I'm not sure if the pain was caused by the class, though, unless I wasn't warmed up enough when I did the poses we tried. Remember, we didn't do a full sequence; we just went into and out of poses for demonstration and learning purposes.

The more likely culprit was that I had a stressful week. My husband had been in the hospital with a blood clot the day before my restorative instruction. All worked out well, but I felt physical stress symptoms I've had under control for quite some time, although this time the symptoms weren't full-blown. I reminded myself to breathe and to engage in helpful, positive self-talk. I worked to stay in the moment and not race ahead with "what if" thoughts. Despite that, throughout Thursday, Friday and intermittently during the weekend, I did have tingling down the left side of my face and left arm and hand throughout Thursday and Friday and intermittently during the weekend. That tingling used to lead to a panic attack or migraine (and it used to be provoked by less stress than I was under this week), but this time it didn't go any further. That is why I suspect my shoulder pain was caused by my body trying to deal with stress as opposed to having been caused by anything I did at class.

When I spoke to Ashley about it, she gave me two yoga stretches to help, massaged the aggravated area, and suggested a hot bath with Epsom salts. All of this helped and by Sunday I was in pretty good shape again. Despite the minor setback, I was again reminded of how much my practice has helped me deal with stress.

I learned the importance of making sure my students are warmed up enough for the poses I plan, which I'm sure will be key as we learn more about sequencing. I also learned about being more proactive in healing my own discomfort (with Ashley's help and advice). Susie says we need to listen to our bodies' whispers, so they don't have to scream to get our attention. I'm learning how to do that and how to show enough kindness (Ahima) to myself to take care of the whispers and the screams.

Fast Forward Four Years

No matter what we do or where we go, we will experience stress in our lives at some time or another. Family members get sick, we lose jobs, relationships change, accidents happen, and work is difficult for a variety of reasons. We can't avoid all stress, but we can process it in ways that help instead of hindering the healing. One helpful thing we can do is self-care. Healthy food, exercise, time to rest, and kindness toward yourself (mental and physical kindness) are a must for all of us. Taking time to take care of yourself at all times, but especially during a period of stress, is very important. You can't help anyone if you don't take care of yourself. Just as important is our attitude towards events or situations. We sometimes add to our stress and suffering by starting a thought process of what "should" or "shouldn't be".

We are much better off accepting the present. Attaching to what was or what we wish something was, causes us pain. Accepting things the way they are and knowing that this experience and the feelings we are having will also change will eventually make those feelings more tolerable. Focusing on what is real can also help us act appropriately for the actual situation. The other thing we do that gets us into trouble during stressful situations is creating every possible scenario that could happen and thinking about "what we would do if".

Our imagination is vast and exceptionally creative. Most things we can imagine will never happen and, contrary to what we think, going through the "what ifs" doesn't prepare us. It causes more stress and suffering, because we are mentally processing difficult events that may never come to be. Even worse, this fruitless mind exercise reduces our ability to cope with what is happening in in front of us. Learning to let go of the "shoulds" and the "what ifs" and focusing on what is happening, with the understanding that it is temporary, helps us to see our options in the moment and allows us to deal with the real stress as opposed to imposed suffering based on what is imagined.

Philosophy

Saturday
12/7/2013

Today Nikki, a Boston based teacher from South Africa, came to our class and spent the day with us teaching philosophy. She is an amazing person and very knowledgeable about "The Bhagavad Gita", which I haven't read yet, and the *Sutras of Pantanjali* (translated by Sri Swami Satchidananda), with which I am more familiar. She radiated peacefulness and such positive energy that everyone immediately felt comfortable with her, and many people opened up on topics held close to their hearts. She listened to their stories and made connections to the story she was telling. It was an emotional day and people shared very private and painful details of their lives and feelings. Nikki was just so warm, and the content connected with people in different ways.

In the "Gita", as she called it, a story is told about a prince who was trying to make sense of our crazy world and to figure out what his path should be and how to follow it. In this story about the human condition, the prince asks Krishna questions such as: "Who am I? Why am I here? What just happened?" and proclaims, "I am lost." I am excited to have the opportunity to find out more and to see if or how the prince answered some of these tough questions about *Dharma*, which is the-way-of-life, or the-essential-nature-of-things. Nikki made the story sound so intriguing and current even though it was written thousands of years ago in a world so different from our own. I can't wait to start reading it!

After learning about the *Gita*, we turned to the *Yoga Sutras of Patanjali*. Earlier in the year I had marked in my own book many of the parts of the sutras that Nikki chose to talk about. This day was amazing. Nikki explained that she was helping to open a crevasse that would let in a little bit of understanding at a time. I picture Nikki with a pickax chipping away. Some of the crevasses would clearly be deep enough for some of us to turn into a rushing torrent of water, maybe even some rapids for a while, until it leads us to calm still waters.

My first teacher, Ally, helped me to form the crevasse, and this led me here to this experience. I wouldn't want this opening to be closed again. This day was hard to put into words, so I'll end here. I have lot to process from this day. I also have a great deal to read and meditate on.

Anusara Yoga and Chakra Workshop

Sunday
12/8/2013

By the end of this session I will have completed 57 hours out of 200. That's amazing! And what a day we had today! Nancy Anger, the owner of "State of Grace" when I took the teacher training, spent the whole day with us to teach us about Anusara Yoga and the Chakras, which are both her specialties.

We were practicing asanas and analyzing poses all morning in an Anusara yoga class. I felt the same connection that I had when we did the Iyengar yoga, but it felt even better. It was a slower practice like the Iyengar, but still physical. We were holding poses longer and concentrating more on the alignment of the body. The difference between this and the Iyengar style was the spirituality of it. We started with chanting, which I have never done before. Even though I love the idea of restorative yoga, this class resonated with me more and, like so many other things I've learned a little about during this course work, I want to find out more, go to some Anusara classes, and see where they will lead.

During the second part of the day, Nancy taught us about the Chakras. I've heard yoga teachers refer to the Chakras, but I hadn't really understood or connected to the ideas about our bodies based on ancient understandings. I guess I am a bit of a skeptic. I am not skeptical about the mind/body connection that the ideas involve; on the contrary; I think the mind has tremendous power over the health and well-being of the body. I guess I am more skeptical about the representation. That doesn't mean I am closed, though. I know I'm probably sounding like a broken record, but this is another aspect of yoga I want to learn more about.

In the afternoon, we took part in an activity to learn about the third chakra by taking turns standing in a circle and sharing several things we love about ourselves. This was to foster self-acceptance. That was harder than it sounds, since women in our society have not traditionally been brought up to speak openly about our best qualities or show self-love. Interestingly, it felt good afterwards. I think everyone should be able to tell a group of people things they like about themselves at least once in their lifetime.

The First Written Test

Friday
12/13/2013

We began the class with two members of the class presenting a sequence that included the Sun Salutation, adding four standing poses. I am amazed at the difference in our confidence when getting up to do this portion of the class, the improvement in our sequencing, and the difference in the amount of constructive criticism we are now giving each other. We are growing, and it is a very obvious change that has taken place since the beginning of this adventure. One of the students who taught tonight is a runner who also teaches spin classes. She had a tremendous amount of energy and when she was done the mood was high in the room. She effectively woke us all up on a Friday night, which can be quite a feat.

Next came our first written test. We expected a multiple-choice test, but it included several short-written responses. There were also several questions for which we were required to match vocabulary to definitions about the Eight Limbs Path, the branches of yoga, and some Sanskrit for good measure. We also had questions about seasonal yoga, anatomy (finding a pose that demonstrated a specific action of muscles) and we had to describe how we would direct someone into two poses. These were all things we went over. It is remarkable to me how much material we have processed in such a short period of time. Susie kept telling us to use the test results as a learning tool by going back and studying those things we struggled with. She told us before the test that she wouldn't be talking about it after we took it and we would get it back in January. I felt OK afterwards, even though I knew I had to go back and reread and study many things, especially the seasonal yoga and some anatomy. Several others, though, were upset. One person spoke for many by saying they underestimated the amount of study needed for the test. The mood and energy that was so high before the test had been completely sucked out of the room. People were quiet and contemplative, and a few were visibly upset.

I came up with two possible concepts that I believe we were supposed to learn from taking this test, aside from the material. First, I think we were supposed to learn a lesson about attachment. According to the Eight Limbs Path, attachment is one of the causes of misery. *Yogis learn how to accept things as they are, feel the feelings they have in the moment, and then let it go.* When people hold onto a specific desired outcome and can't accept a different outcome (like not doing well on a test), they become more upset than they need to be. The test didn't cause the misery; the thoughts that followed the event caused the misery. Thoughts like: "I should have done better" (shoulds), "They didn't tell us how to prepare" (blame), "I must be stupid" (judgment). Our own thoughts, which we have control of, are what truly cause a lot of our unhappiness.

Eleanor Roosevelt said, "No one can make you feel inferior without your consent." I used to be prone to self-judging thoughts, but yoga has helped me so much with that. I was also overly worried about what others might think and I would obsess over it (again, this was my doing, not theirs). That was just another form of self-judgment. At the beginning it seemed impossible to shoo those thoughts away. However, by learning to take responsibility and doing what I needed to fix a situation without judgmental thoughts (and replacing them with more positive thoughts), the negativity is almost never a part of my self-talk anymore. It does take time and effort, but it is worth it. I can cope with events that happen with a much clearer head, and even when I am sad or stressed I still know I can do what it takes to get through. Life is hard enough without adding to our misery by attaching ourselves to negative thoughts, or a single outcome that may or may not play out.

I believe that the second concept we were to learn was that what we are doing is hard and what we are doing is important. Both make it worth doing and worth putting the effort into. I also learned that I have a lot of material to review and remember.

After the test one student did breathe-work. He taught the breath of fire. He has an incredibly calming voice and I could picture him leading a meditation class. I found the breath of fire challenging because I became a little light-headed and uncomfortable. I will have to learn to be more comfortable with breath work in general. I will also have to learn a lot more about it. Maybe that would help. If I understood more about the premises, benefits and strategies I would feel more comfortable.

Later in the evening we went over several balance poses, and we were given an assignment to read more about them and of course practice. I came home exhausted but happy that I'm more than 60 hours down. I'm learning, growing, seeing new possibilities, and moving closer every day to the goal of completing this course.

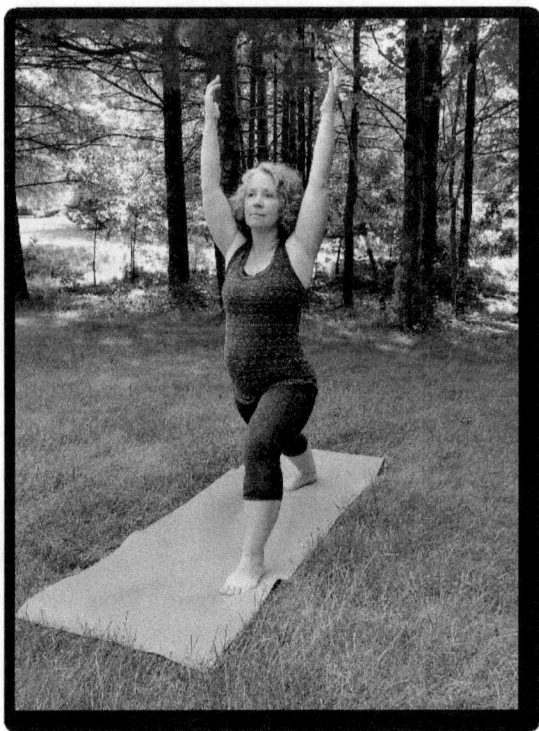

Virabhadrasana I   Warrior I

Sound Healing

Friday
12/20/2013

Tonight, we came to a class that was advertized as a "Sound Healing" class at our studio. This was open to the public. A group called Soundscapers Services came to the studio to lead a guided meditation involving the use of drums, shakers of all kinds, bells, Tibetan bowls, crystal bowls, a gong, a didgeridoo, and other instruments I couldn't see or identify, as we had our eyes closed in meditation once the program started. The idea was that vibrations and sounds can be healing to the mind, spirit, and body. The drumming and chanting seemed to have roots in many different ancient traditions. If you are interested, you can find more information online about sound healing and the benefits of meditation.

I have never had an experience quite like this one. First, the narrator told us a little about what his organization does and the instruments they use. He also had us introduce ourselves and share whether we had any intention for the night. I just intended to try to stay open to this new experience and learn something from it. Many people were there specifically looking for some kind of healing, either physical or emotional. During this yoga course I have found many people who seem so well put together are seeking peace or healing. It just shows that we are the same in many ways and that we all suffer some times. I believe, though, that we sometimes think that no one else will understand, and that our suffering is somehow different from others'.

Well, I'm sure no suffering is exactly the same, just as each of us is different in many ways, but learning to move on and let go of suffering is a part of life we all share. We all suffer and handle it in productive or non-productive ways. Hearing so many stories from so many people who are deeply affected by issues in their lives (many of whom have similar issues to my own), I am realizing more and more how connected we are, yet how separate we sometimes make ourselves as we go about our daily lives. I think we need to learn how to connect to each other again even though we allow our lives to get so crazy. I think I need to let enough go so that I can find more time for real connections. Anyway, I'm sure this theme will come up again. Let's get back to the class.

The program started with a loud, pounding drumbeat and loud, harsh shaker sounds. The vibrations were so strong they could be felt through the floor. They seemed to bounce off the walls and through the inside of my chest, bouncing from rib to rib and the back of my sternum. The vibrations seemed to fill the space where my heart is. We started out standing and moving but quickly moved to a reclining position with blankets, pillows, and bolsters.

After that, the leader took us through a vivid guided imagery sequence of the kind you might learn in a relaxation course. As he spoke, the room filled with different sounds from the vast variety of percussion instruments, bowls, the didgeridoo, and voices. In hypnotic tones, our guide walked us through a green field on a dark night with a sky full of stars. He led us though a pathway to a beautiful stream where we dipped our feet and legs in the cool stream as outside debris, such as sticks and leaves, were washed away downstream by the water. Next, any internal debris we had, such as emotional or physical issues that we should let go of, were washed downstream by the water. All the while the music continued and changed as we moved into a deeper meditation.

As the program progressed, I experienced a great range of sensations. The music was all around us and seemed to be coming from all directions. At times, the musicians must have been walking right next to us, but absent was the sense of a person moving into my space that I would usually feel when someone nears my yoga mat. I only felt the music and the reactions of my body and mind. At one point I realized there were tears running down the sides of my face. I was not really crying, but tears were flowing gently wetting my cheeks. After that, I felt like I was melting into the floor. I felt somewhat disconnected from my body even though by this time I was uncomfortably cold and shivering. (I don't think the room was cold, and I had one yoga blanket under me on my yoga mat and another fleece blanket over me. I also wore a fleece sweater.) Despite the shivering, I felt the sensation of my arms, legs and torso melting into the floor beneath me.

Later in the two-hour program, I had the sensation of being in a deep meditation with the above feeling, yet I was acutely aware of some uncomfortable sensations in my body. Besides feeling cold, I felt a pulsing pain in several parts of the right side of my body. In a line, I had five points of pain; first in my right knee, then just off the side of my right hip, then in my chest, then in my collar bone, and lastly in my right armpit. As the music softened and we were led back out of the visualization and came back to the room, most of the sensations had passed. The pain in my armpit and the feeling of being cool (although no longer shivering) lasted for a little while after the experience.

In the end I felt quiet at first, then uncomfortable. Toward the end of the class, the guide passed an African talking stick and gave everyone the opportunity to say something if they wished. At that point, I felt an urge to just get out of there. It isn't that I didn't find it an extraordinary experience, but I think I was just overstimulated.

Some participants talked about a sense of peace and spoke beautifully about how they felt and what they had gained from the experience. Many people looked very peaceful and grateful. I thought I was the only person in the room who didn't feel completely at peace, but then at my weekly yoga class another member described herself as "wigged out" and said she had wanted to get out of there, too. I took some comfort in knowing I wasn't the only one who didn't feel peaceful.

Despite my urge to leave the room, I waited for the entire class to speak and the session to be complete. As I drove home, I had moments of anger and a few moments of tears. I let those feelings pass. Eventually those feelings left me during my 20-minute drive home and I just felt quiet.

Fast Forward Four Years

The uncomfortable feeling during and after the sound healing session puzzled me at the time. I also had two other instances during this teacher training class in which I became very uncomfortable during activities that other people seemed to enjoy and find pleasurable. I was puzzled and probably did some self-blaming: *Maybe I wasn't focused enough, maybe I did the breathing exercise wrong*, etc. The point was that I thought it was me and me alone. Whenever you hear about meditative practices, you hear about how relaxing, calming, and soothing they can be, so when I didn't have that experience, I felt like I might have been doing something wrong.

Judging a reaction or feeling is the first mistake. We should always accept our feelings. Feelings are not good or bad. They are just something to be noticed. What you should know, though, is that everyone doesn't react the same way and there are times when meditation, breathing exercises, and even asanas can have different effects on people.

I accepted that and let go of the judgment. However, an article featured in the May 2018 issue of *Yoga Journal* recently caught my eye. It was called, *The Dark Side of Meditation*, by Jessica Downey. In the article, the author wrote that many people, especially those who have experienced some past trauma, sometimes have a hard time with meditation. In my case, during the sound healing, my reaction was uncomfortable, but the discomfort passed. For some people, however, this reaction can re-traumatize the person meditating. The article was based on people's personal experiences and data collected from practitioners. I highly recommend *Yoga Journal,* and I highly recommend checking out this article.

I'm certainly not saying to stay away from meditation. Many people derive great peace and calm from this practice. A lot of practitioner's experience stress relief, clarity, and many positive effects from meditation. I'm just cautioning against a one-size-fits-all approach to any form of yoga. I believe yoga asanas, breathing exercises, and meditation help us release trauma and stress and allow us to let go of things we don't need any more.

Just be aware. Be mindful and accepting of the experiences you have and make decisions about your practice based on your physical and emotional needs.

Also, use this same awareness as you survey your yoga class as a teacher. Since my training, I have tried meditation for short periods and for me that was a good place to start. As a practitioner and/or a yoga teacher, you should be aware that people may have different responses and that emotions can come up during contemplative, meditative, movement, and breathing exercises.

Look for practices that meet your needs and expectations and be aware and accepting of how you feel. If a practice isn't working for you, search for something else. Seek medical help if needed. If teaching, look for signs that students are comfortable, calm, and reacting well to the practice. Offer ways out, such as keeping their eyes open, and talk to participants afterward, especially if you note someone struggling. Remember that everyone is different and that there isn't a right or wrong way to react to meditation. Accept where you are (or where your students are) and make decisions from there as to how best to proceed.

There are many books available that describe the various ways to meditate for beginners. There are also phone apps available that can lead you in meditation, guided imagery and breathing exercises. Check out these resources to find something that meets your needs and interests.

Yoga Instruction
My First Two-Hours of Teaching

Friday
12/27/2013

This week, as I had time off from class and work during the holidays, I spent some time working on my yoga class. I studied areas I needed to work on based on the test we took a couple of weeks ago, I worked on the balance poses for our next class, and I've done some reading in and outside of my teaching manual. I've also started my 10 hours of teaching, which is required outside of class. I began with my family, which may sound like the easy way to go, except that my husband and daughter make up a tough crowd. I started with them first for convenience, but also because I knew they would be honest as to whether I am ready to try a class with other people. When I directed my daughter in doing the Sun Salutation, she told me, "Your voice wasn't loud enough, and you didn't sound confident." It was exactly what I needed to hear again as I practiced because, without honest feedback, I wouldn't improve. My family is very supportive and will help me any way they can. Their honesty helped me get a true sense of how I was doing.

The two, hour long classes I did with them were geared toward beginning level yoga students as my husband, Bob, had never done yoga before, and I focused the poses on flexibility and strength. Both my husband and daughter, Catherine, are athletes. They both run long distances, bike, and ski. Bob plays tennis and Cat swims on her school team. She has done a little yoga in the past, but she likes a higher pace in her activities at the moment. During her vacation, she was working with an injured foot, which limited her motion for anything requiring being on the ball of her foot. Because of his athletics, Bob had some tightness in his hips, spine, and hamstrings. Meeting these needs and learning what poses would work was a challenge. I reviewed the recommended sequence of activity and pose types in my manual, and then I prepped the area.

The first hour-long session was more challenging because I discovered how long it takes to teach poses, correct alignment, give feedback, and see what poses worked best with my current students. In my own practice, I can do a lot more poses and I can run through them much more quickly. That makes sense since I don't have to demo and explain the poses to myself as I go through a sequence, and I know how each pose feels in my own body and what I need next. With my "students" I had to watch for signs of strain and stress, like tightness in the jaw, heavier breathing, alignment that showed tightness, etc.

The next session was a bit easier. I was more confident, the sequence was better, and I was more prepared with props for Bob to help make the poses more gentle, accessible, and restorative. I had to encourage him to hold back because he kept saying he could go farther, but I could see alignment issues and signs of stress. Be careful with competitive people. With the props, he was a little more relaxed. The second session was better sequenced, and I was amazed again how quickly the time went and how ready my students were for savasana. Afterwards, I did get positive feedback from both Bob and Cat, although

Bob was sore for the next couple of days. Catherine said I sounded more confident and that I was loud enough this time. She even agreed to ask a couple of her friends to come over soon to participate in another class that I could teach and use for hour number three. Next week or the week after, my instructors will be focusing on sequencing, which will again make it easier to plan a sequence to meet a given purpose. That will make my next hours more focused, organized, and cohesive.

To complete the 10 hours of teaching I have several volunteers, including some of my daughter's friends and some of my friends who will do more hours for me if needed. I have a lot of people who have said they wouldn't mind trying an hour of class for me. The trick will be scheduling it around everyone's busy schedules.

I am amazed at how much I have learned so far and how much more confident I've gotten in the teaching part of yoga. I'm not even halfway there and I've come so far. It will be interesting to see where all of this will lead.

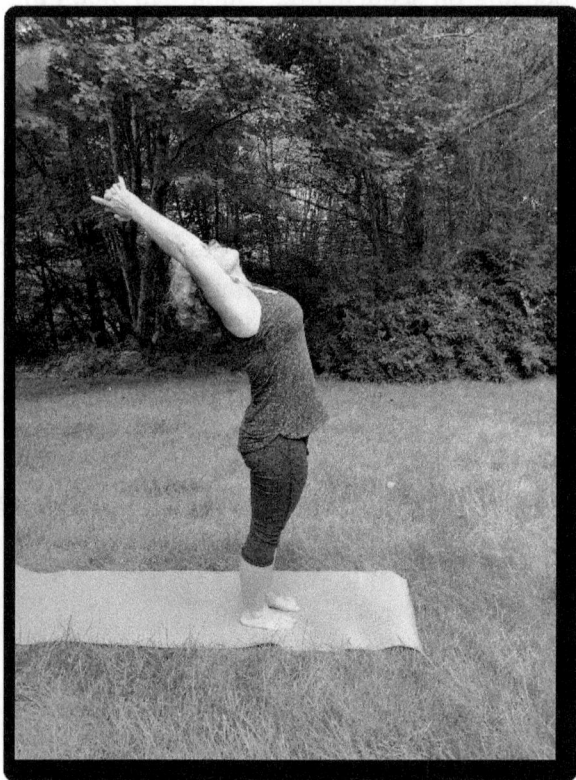

Urdhva Hastasana   Upward Salute

Compassion

Sunday
12/29/2013

In addition to the work I did for this course this week, I've been doing some related reading to satisfy my own interests in the study of yoga. I read two texts related to compassion and recommend them both. The first was a chapter in the book "Living Your Yoga", by Judith Lasatar. The second was an article from the December 2013 *Yoga Journal* entitled *Wisdom*, by Sally Kempton. Everything they wrote about connected to the Yamas of the Eight Limbs Path of Yoga as compassionate actions that are non-harming and honest.

Compassion is also related to the Five Afflictions described by Patanjali in the Sutras, which include *spiritual ignorance, pride, desire/attachment, aversion,* and *fear.* Any one or all can keep us from acting compassionately at times. Attachment to outcomes and fear can cause us to act in ways we believe are compassionate yet may be wrong. Both texts gave me a lot to think about and process. I'm sure my views will change as I continue to learn, but this is what I believe now.

True compassion comes only when we are present in the moment and we can see a situation for what it is and remain unattached to the outcome. If a parent sees their child about to touch a hot stove, the compassionate thing to do is to stop him, even if it means scaring him in the process. In the dangerous moment, the adult isn't worried about upsetting the child; she is set on preventing a burn at all costs. In that example it is easy to see the compassionate choice, but what if that child is older and is using drugs, stealing from the family and acting out in dangerous ways? What is the best way to really have compassion for all impacted? What help is available? There is no "right" answer here, by the way. Different families could make different "right" decisions for themselves.

The answers can only be found in the moment and with an unclouded view of the situation. If the parent is driven by fear or attachment—fear of losing the child if he decides to refuse treatment, or if his behavior is self-destructive, fear of others finding out that her child has that kind of problem, attachment to the child's acceptance or positive reactions, then it will be harder for the parent to be present and make the best decision - the most compassionate decision - for herself and her child. Judith Lasater pointed out that fear is usually related to the past (we fear what has happened to us before), and the future (we fear what might happen). Fear prevents us from being in the moment and prevents us from seeing a situation for what it really is.

When we are afraid in the present, we deal with it (i.e. immediately stopping the child when he is about to touch the stove). When the thing we are afraid of has passed or hasn't happened yet (for example, "What if she..."), we can't deal with it (because it is not real), but it can cloud our judgment and make us suffer. I think many of us are good at making ourselves suffer with worrying and inventing scenarios that might happen.

To be truly compassionate we must also be able is to see our connection to others. When we can see how connected we are to other people and understand that we are the same in many ways and that we could at some point find ourselves in the other person's circumstances, we find more compassion. Illness, grief, dependency, and poverty are all part of life as humans. Any of us could find ourselves in positions where any of those things might impact our lives or the lives of those we love. If we understand that we are not that different from others who are suffering, then we can better find the connection that allows us to feel empathy, which may lead to compassionate action.

I also believe that we sometimes lack compassion at times for others, because they represent things we don't like in ourselves. So, think about this. If we can forgive ourselves for our shortcomings and perceived flaws, maybe we would be more open to having compassion to others. But first, of course, we need to be able to forgive ourselves.

Remember that the Yamas don't just apply to others! We need to be non-harming, caring, honest, etc., to ourselves as well. This means we can only do what we can do. If you do your best, even if you fail, you did all you could do, and that should bring some contentment instead of judgment. Make a plan for improvement but leave the self-judgment behind. Mistakes mean we are human, not that we are lacking in some way.

Don't get me wrong; I don't think that non-judgment of self is easy, but it is important that we try, and I'm working on it. This is important because I believe we need to show compassion and kindness to ourselves before we can show compassion to others. If we don't take care of ourselves, we will not have the strength, patience, and love left over to act compassionately toward others. Instead, we will develop resentment, and if we continue to serve only someone else's needs while that resentment builds, then we are not being very honest with ourselves.

As I read the Lasater and Kempton texts, the words gave me a lot to think about. Doors open for us all the time if we live in the present, so we shouldn't get discouraged the next time something "terrible" happens. If we live in the moment, we can find ways to deal with difficult times more compassionately.

Saturday
1/18/2014

Today we had another class with Nikki who earlier taught our class yoga philosophy. She really simplified the whole idea of compassion. She is amazing and sees things so clearly.

First, she said that, "Everything we need to answer any question or problem we have is inside us already." If we are asking for advice, we are likely to be looking for validation of what we already "know" to be true. I think that goes with what I said above about living in the moment. If you aren't in the moment, your view of this will be clouded. I know I have trouble trusting that I really do have the answers, but maybe if I was focusing on the moment, some of the self-doubt would pass faster.

Second, she said there is a quote by Buddha that says, "Don't take away my suffering." If you take away someone else's suffering, you may also take away their opportunity to deal with the experience of healing and letting go. Be there for them and listen to them, but you can't fix their problems.

Lastly, she gave a definition of compassion that she learned from one of her teachers. Compassion is:1. Knowing where someone is at a given time, 2. Understanding what it took for them to get there, and 3. Not helping unless they ask you to".

Fast Forward Four Years

Compassion

Many people I know, including me, tend to want to "fix" things for people. I believe education and other helping professions attract fixers, but many other people also have that tendency. We can't let a problem lie and we feel compelled to give our opinion (often unsolicited) even when we should be silent. It can be difficult to just listen and wait for someone to ask for assistance or our opinion, but I have come to believe that it is prudent to do that most of the time. We are all coming from different places, and if you recognize that everyone has a light inside of them, then you can recognize that they have the ability to make the best choices when they tap into that light. I still must work hard to listen; of course, I sometimes fail at it, but with practice it is getting easier. I have come to believe Nikki's definition of compassion and I think it is important enough to keep up the effort to live it even though it is against my natural tendency.

.

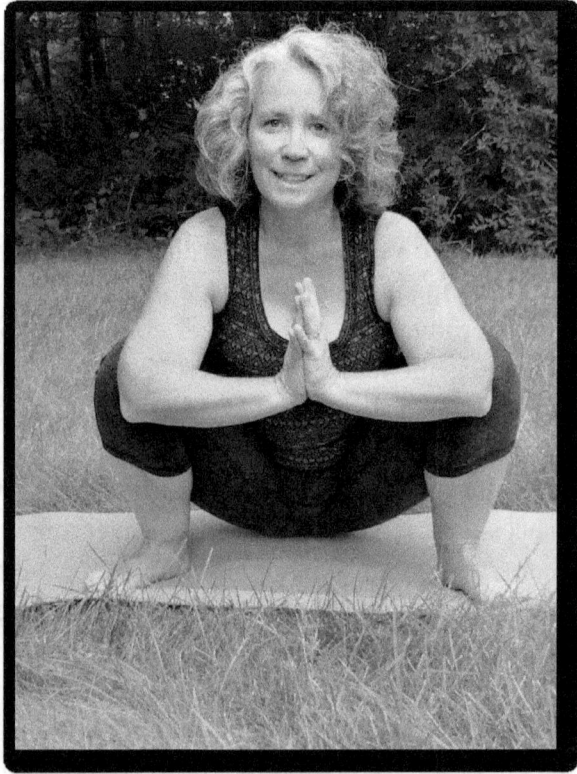

Malasana   Garland Pose

Yoga Instruction:
My Third Hour of Teaching

Friday
1/3/2014

I started the New Year right by teaching another hour-long class. This time, though, I didn't teach my family. Catherine had texted two friends who agreed to come with their siblings to be students in the class. I expected four teenagers, but I was surprised when five teenagers and one adult appeared for class. The adult was the mother of two of the young participants, and she happened to be a fitness instructor. I was a little intimidated and space was a little tight, but all went well, and once the class got started, I relaxed and enjoyed myself. I did keep my notes for the sequence close at hand even though I had practiced and reviewed it repeatedly, including reviewing my class book about setting up and reviewing important descriptions of each pose. I knew that this would be a beginner's class and I geared it that way, even though the adult had some yoga experience.

Because I was working with teens, I had planned several partner poses, as I thought they would be fun for the girls. This worked out very well. Two sisters gave each other a bit of a hard time during one of them, but it seemed to be all in good fun. Once I started, it was easy to see the needs and I added extra demos and modeling to help with alignment and proper transitioning. I was able to answer many questions easily and felt confident in correcting misalignment. The sequence worked out well, as I taught several poses in the warm up that I used in the Sun Salutation in the middle of practice, so when we started to flow a little, poses were at least a bit familiar.

We repeated the Sun Salutation twice for each side, adding standing poses with the repetition. The balance poses were a little difficult, but with the modifications (toe on the floor for eagle) and partner activities (dancer palm to palm facing one another), everyone could participate, and they seemed to have fun. I did some slower poses for a cool down, including bridge and a reclined twist, and then went into *Savasana*. which was difficult for two of the girls and afterwards I talked to them about strategies to help them relax and focus on their breath and body, including arm positioning, placing hands or a sandbag on the belly to help draw attention to the breath, etc.

After the class, the kids rushed upstairs to where my daughter had juice and fresh baked cookies waiting for them, and the parent came and talked to me a little about the class. She suggested sitting in on other yoga classes and taking notes and writing down verbiage for giving clearer directions for some poses. She also said she would come back with the girls again for more classes to give me more practice. When I asked Catherine what her friends said about the class, she quoted them as saying it was "fun and hard". One, in true teenage form, called me a "yoga master". I was happy to receive the undeserved praise and was glad that they enjoyed the class and were willing to come back.

Sanskrit and Revolved Poses

Friday
1/17/2014

Parivrkta, Parsarata, Parsva (with a "szh" sound for the s), Utthitta...tonight reminded me of sitting in my freshman Spanish I class in high school. Boy, that is going back a little bit! Anyway, we spent time learning some more basic Sanskrit and we practiced using it with more confidence. It will be a process. (That reminder is more for me than for anyone else!) I have been trying to practice the names of some of the poses we have learned in the past weeks, but as I've added more poses, some of the elements have been getting mixed up in my mind. Not to worry, though; Ashley introduced us to "Sanskrit Man".

Sanskrit Man was in our teacher's manual all the time, but I hadn't given him the proper respect before tonight. I will have to spend more time getting to know him. He is a man with all of the Sanskrit names that represent all of the body parts that move in yoga. My hope is that if I can connect the names of the parts to the names of the poses (which at times include the body part), then I will experience clarity. An example of one pose that works this way is "*Janu Sirsasana*" (*Janu*=knee, Sirsa=head, *Asana*=pose).

Other key words are related to directionality or relationships in addition to body parts, such as *Tadasana Urdhva Hastasana* (*Urdva*=upward, *Hasta*=hand/arm, *Asana*=pose).   Still others are related to animals or shapes that the pose is named after, such as *Navasana* (*Nav*=boat, asana=pose) and *Garudasana* (*Garud*=Eagle and asana= pose).

While my classmates and I tried to name the poses in Namaskar B (Sun Salutation B), our teacher Susie flowed gracefully through the poses, only stopping and freezing when we could not come up with the name. This was a lot of fun and quite a learning experience to see how the body is supposed to be aligned during those poses. I realized that I needed to make more flash cards in the next week. The evening really helped, though, and now I know that I will need to learn a great deal of the Sanskrit names. Susie explained to us that learning some basic Sanskrit and the Sanskrit names for common poses is a sign of respect for the ancient practice of yoga that we are learning, even if we don't always use these names in a class we teach. Susie suggested using a site on "You Tube" that reviews the names so that we can listen and develop the proper pronunciation.

After this, one of my classmates led us in a breathing activity with lovely imagery, which seemed like it would be very good to help people with busy minds get centered and focused on the practice and their body. It is hard for some people to quiet their mind, but this visualization could help settle someone's thoughts.

She started by asking us to visualize a five-point star. Then she suggested we imagine our breath as we inhale moving up the first point of the star and coming down to the center of the star as we exhaled. Then, with each breath, move up and down from tip to center along each point of the star until again reaching the top. Her timing was incredible, and the visualization was beautiful and calming - very good for centering. I'm learning the breathing techniques, but I'd never seen or heard of this one, and I'm glad this classmate chose to share it with us. Clearly, we all have something inside us that is worth sharing with others.

Later in the evening we practiced some revolved (twisting) poses and I do need more practice with these. I think the problem is not so much my flexibility as my focus and therefore my balance. Along with practice with Namaskar B this week, which was our assignment, I will need to practice the two revolved poses to improve my balance.

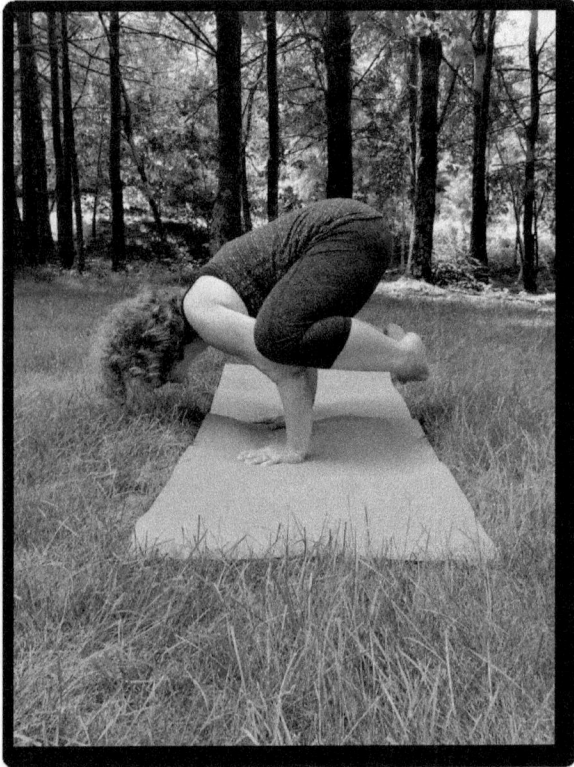

Bakasana   Crane/Crow Pose

Sequencing, Assists, and Inversions

Sunday
1/19/2014

This all-day Sunday class was another very physical day, but the level of activity made the time go fast. We learned more about sequencing. The book approach that I had looked at previously to plan my classes that I've taught so far was pretty general, but Ashley and Susie gave us an important point to consider for designing a sequence that made a lot of sense to me. They suggested first to decide your peak pose in the sequence and then build the poses you would use before and after based on the physical needs of that pose. For example, if a peak pose needs open hips, then plan poses and actions with the same opening and stretching needed to help slowly open the hips in preparation for that pose. That makes sense, right?

I believe I did that to some extent when I taught the larger class with my daughter's friends, I repeated postures and added on to repeated sequences, but I don't think I always chose poses with similar shapes and similar actions that lead up to any given pose. During this class we worked together in groups. Each group was given a peak pose, and they had to develop a short sequence to prepare for it. We did OK in the limited amount of time we had, but I'm anxious to try it both on my own and with a group of volunteers.

During class, we revisited assists, which was needed because earlier we didn't have as much understanding of the poses and the anatomy of the poses that we have now. We also practiced touching other people yesterday in the all-day session about Thai Yoga Massage, which really took away some inhibitions. Learning how to be comfortable touching people you don't know very well for assists, massage, etc. doesn't come naturally and feels a little awkward at first—at least it did for me, even though I do tend to touch when I talk or hug someone in distress. Having a lot of practice lately with touching in this context does make that part easier. Not that we still don't have a long way to go with learning appropriate assists, but I think that, overall, we were able to understand how assists work and we can see the benefit of them. My partner was great, and, with her feedback, I started to see how helpful some of the assists could be for other people and for me.

Twice today I learned first-hand how great an assist could be. First, in my regular yoga class, Susie helped me deeper into a twist. It felt so good, and I had no idea my body could move as deeply into the twist as I did with her help. Now I know how it feels and I can work towards that motion on my own. The second assist from Susie I had tonight was even more amazing—although maybe *amazing* isn't a strong enough word. That happened when we started talking about inversions at the end of class and Susie helped me into a headstand.

I have never done a headstand and I was quite scared to try one. At the beginning of the instructor's course, Susie asked us to think about a pose that scares us and then to try to be open to doing it eventually, or at least begin developing some of the poses that build strength for that scary pose. I had been thinking about it since then, so when she asked who wanted to come up into a headstand, I timidly started to walk forward. Someone else volunteered more assertively, but a classmate behind me then called out, "Lisa, do you want to do a headstand?" The other classmate bowed out to let me go first, and Susie guided me into a headstand by talking me through the steps and supporting my legs.

The world looks and feels very different upside down the first time you try! It was a little disorienting, but I was so excited that I was willing to try it and that I had a trustworthy teacher who was willing to help me. I will be practicing it and I will eventually have that pose as a part of my regular practice. Knowing how that felt—getting into a pose safely that I may not have been able to attempt or hold on my own, with help from someone I trusted, gave me the confidence to learn more independently, knowing how it felt to do the pose. I expect that having that experience will make me more willing to give someone else an assist to gain confidence in a difficult or scary pose.

Fast Forward Four Years

That moment of going up in a headstand is still an amazing one. Since then I have learned to do an independent headstand only later to be advised by my doctor not to do them because I had moderate arthritis in my neck. Everything changes. Assists can be exhilarating, but I caution against using them without being sure of your purpose and remember that one size doesn't fit all. Be sure that you have the knowledge, skill, and strength to do the assist appropriately, and know your students' abilities and flexibility. Also, be aware that some people have an adverse reaction to being touched. In an adult yoga class, I taught at my school, we worked up to Warrior III and I assisted a couple of students who didn't think they could balance in the pose. They were grateful and felt good that they could find some balance in a difficult, new pose. In another class I was a participant in, the teacher chose to give everyone an assist to lower students' hips during child's pose by putting pressure on the students' lower backs. One student yelled out in pain, because he was not flexible enough to go into that expression of the pose yet. Be focused, purposeful, and cautious when doing assist.

This made it clear that a yoga teacher's first responsibility is to be aware of the student's ability and limitations while teaching and be willing to adjust the lesson to their needs and levels and not blindly follow a lesson plan for the sake of the plan itself, which of course, is exactly what I do every day while teaching my second-grade students in the classroom.

Ripples in the Pond

Friday
1/24/2014

Our guest teacher, Nikki (Philosophy and Thai Yoga Massage), talked about everything we do in life causing ripples in the pond; we may never see where the ripples go or how far they may eventually move from the start. She connected that to our Teacher Training Program, and I can really relate to that. My study of yoga has already changed my perspective on life and made me much calmer, happier, and more at ease. The ripples of that have been and will continue to be far reaching. I think without the change of perspective I would not have been able to stay in my current job and I may not have been able to learn to control the anxiety that was taking so much joy out of my life by directing my attention away from events and people so important to me. And I am sure these changes in me are having a positive impact on those around me, as ripples in the pond that expand outward beyond my personal horizon and beyond my imagination.

I have no idea where the personal growth that I've already experienced will lead. I'm getting stronger, more flexible and healthier. I'm learning more and more about the philosophy that I believe has changed my life. I've met new and amazing people and made connections that I never would have imagined. I've already begun to see ripples that I could not have imagined or expected. After teaching my third yoga class, I was asked to consider working with a high school cross country team to incorporate yoga into their training during the summer. The kids are great and I'm looking forward to that opportunity.

Later, when I heard one of my classmates ask our teacher about information on yoga for runners, I jumped in and asked for the same. As a result, the other student asked me if I'd like to co-teach or assist in two community center yoga classes for athletes training for a triathlon. Although that scares me, I agreed. I would have never imagined myself doing anything like that.

Will I ever teach yoga regularly? Who knows? Will I ever take money to teach yoga? I'm not really sure. Will I use what I've learned to live better and help friends and family? Yes. Will my life change in ways that I never imagined? Absolutely. Whatever comes, I really don't feel attached to the outcome. If I'm too tied to an outcome, I may miss an opportunity I didn't expect to come along.

For me, this is the essence of practicing yoga and a major shift in my perspective and understanding that brings me closer to my "perfect self", which is hidden within and barricaded from discovery by ego and thoughts that cause suffering.

Fast Forward Four Years

As it turned out, because of schedules, timing, etc., working with the cross-country team never panned out. I have however taught a session of yoga for beginners at the public library, I have taught many sessions after school at my school for teachers in our district, and I occasionally volunteer to teach for a community yoga project a couple of my classmates run locally. I even taught a few private sessions for a friend for which I was paid for the first and only time so far. At this time, I don't feel I have time to teach yoga year-round with my teaching schedule and family obligations, but I still love to have some low-pressure opportunities to teach.

I also hope that when I teach these volunteer classes, there might be some ripples in the pond that are farther reaching than I am aware. Maybe my action is helping someone else. It is OK if I never know.

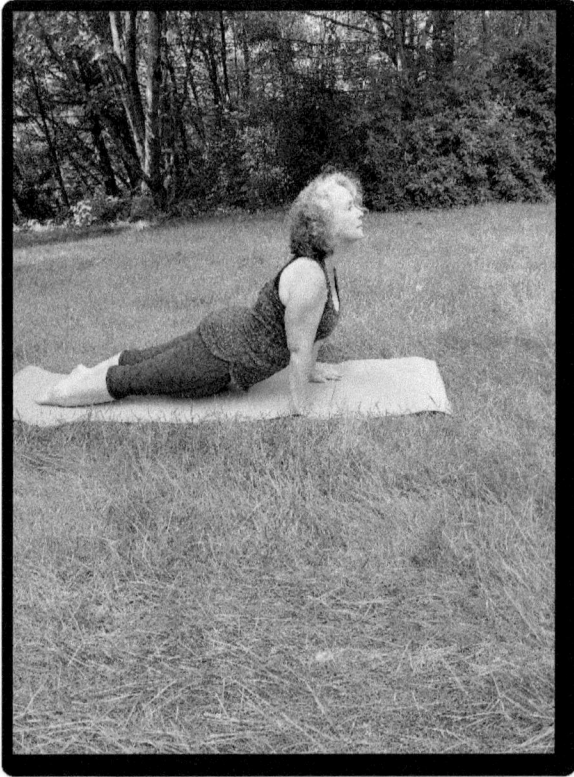

Urdhva Mukha Svanasana
Upward Facing Dog

The Gunas, Revolved Poses, and More Inversions

Friday
1/24/2014

After Nikki had finished her talk about ripples on the pond, we continued with more yoga philosophy. Susie taught us about the *Gunas*, which are how the "ancient systems of yoga defined three qualities of nature that bind us to the material universe".

The Gunas three qualities of nature describe the tendencies or states of people and things in the universe and impact how they experience and interact with the universe. These qualities are changing, and one person can go through all of these qualities at different moments, but people tend to gravitate toward one or the other at different times in their lives or throughout their lives. The first state is *Rajas*, which is associated with fire, passion, high activity, and heat. People or things in a *Rajas* state are non-stop, busy, and/or active. They may tend to be quick tempered. The second is the *Tamas* state in which people appear to be idle, tend towards darkness or dullness, and/or appear more sedentary. They may tend toward depression. At this state, a person may need more comforting and nurturing. People in a Rajas state can sometimes burn themselves out and end up in a Tamas state. The third state, *Sattva* associated with a lightness of being, serenity, and a feeling of well-being. This state is very desirable, but the danger is feeling smug or distant from others. It is believed that we move back and forth between these states and that our goal should be self-awareness and the ability to manage and balance our tendencies.

Later, we worked on two revolved poses—revolved chair (*Parivrtta Utkatasana*) and revolved side-angle (*Parivrtta Parsvakonasana*), and I volunteered to teach these two poses to the class next week. I'll need to practice in front of people every chance I get. I need to work on the revolved poses, and this will give me practice.

We finished the night with inversions. First, we practiced supported shoulder stands. We started with three blankets as props under our back to support our necks. I found that three blankets were very uncomfortable for me since I am small, and my neck ended up in an awkward position. I tried again with two blankets and that was much better. My shoulder stand needs more practice, though, as I'm not able to do it very well without support. First, though, I'm determined to master the headstand. I've been practicing the headstand since last week's class when Susie helped me up. I'm beginning to connect more to my core and I am getting up more easily, but without the wall I can't stay there yet. I seem to need at least one foot on the wall to stay up at all. I'll keep at it and Susie and Ashley offered to help people who wanted to work on that if we came to any of their classes.

As I continue to practice my shoulder stand, I will keep in mind Susie's admonition: "You teach from where you are." That means you may not be able to do every pose there is, but as a teacher, your job is to continue learning and to grow.

Our Thirteenth Friday Class

Friday
1/31/2014

If I've calculated right, we are about halfway through our 200-hours. I am really doing this, and it is going relatively quickly. I am working hard, though. It is still hard to balance home, work, and things I want to do for the class. I've been trying to study and practice the poses in addition to the new things we are learning. I'm also trying to get through a book about yoga as part of an athlete's training to prepare for the two classes designed for a group of half-marathon runners that I agreed to teach with one of my yoga instructor friends.

I also need to start planning the full class I will be teaching as a final project for my training. I can use a similar sequence to any I have already prepared. As I look at these sequences, I need to make sure the poses build to prepare for a key peak pose and then wind down. I think I may be making too much of this. I've been planning my own sequences for 3-4 times a week of home practice for a couple of years now. I realized the pattern I used wasn't much different from the recommended sequences, but I don't necessarily gear my sequences fully towards a theme or building towards a peak pose. I think I just have to start writing down a couple of possible sequences, so I'll stop putting it off and obsessing over it.

Tonight, our class was very small; there were only 16 out of the usual 21 participants and Ashley. We missed those who weren't there. It was very different with so many people missing, but it was a quiet, calm night. It felt more relaxed even though we got a lot done. We started with *Kapalabhati* breathing, which involves passive inhaling and forceful exhaling, with the abdominal muscles forcing short breaths out. After that, we taught the poses that were assigned to us last week. I taught the revolved chair (*Parivrkta Uktinasana*), moving into a revolved side angle (*Parivrkta Parsvakonasana*).

Some of the revolved poses are difficult for me because they require significantly more balance and flexibility of the torso than I have at this time. I volunteered to teach these poses to force myself to master them and other revolved poses. These poses are hard to teach due to the different directions involving rights and lefts and mirroring, which is a challenge. Was that my right and your left? Or the other way around?

I practiced and felt prepared, but I felt like I was going too slowly during the teaching because I had to think carefully about every direction. I did it, though, and it was one more time practicing in front of a group, which will make it easier the next time. A couple of things I have to remember is consistently cueing people to lengthen before twisting and to straighten the gaze (neck position) before having them step back or move leg positions.

After we all tried teaching one of the groups, we reviewed and practiced some seated poses. I've met a new challenge pose

86

(aside from a headstand and a shoulder stand); it is *Gomukhasana* (cow face pose). I just don't like it, even though I grew up in a farm with cows. The fact that I don't like it, though, means it is something I should be practicing. I need to work on the arm position as well as settling my bottom flat on the floor with my legs all twisted. I'll get there. This clearly involves a different part of the hip than pigeon and other hip openers I have no trouble with.

At the end of class, we continued working on the headstand and supported shoulder stand. We assisted each other, and I got close to the headstand again. I'll keep at it. Ashley also taught us a chair assist for the supported shoulder stand that was really amazing. It looked uncomfortable but felt wonderful. You got the feeling of being in the inversion without needing the same balance and strength to get there.

Next week Susie will run the class and we'll do more seated poses and learn more about meditation. Right now, though, I'm feeling unmotivated and unbalanced. I guess I'm in a *Tamas state* if I apply the Gunas we learned last week. I do sometimes tend towards that direction, especially when my expectations for work and how much needs to get done are set too high. I think I start out in a *Rajas state* (kind of hot and maybe frenzied and super motivated), but then burn myself out for a bit. I'll need to work toward some balance. Maybe I should relax a little tonight. I may not finish everything I intended to do, and that needs to be OK. I've got to let go of unreasonable expectations.

Fast Forward Four Years

Using positive self-talk, letting go of unreasonable expectations, and trying to focus on the present has been critical to my ability to stay positive, stay balanced, and avoid upset in our chaotic world. It is still a process, but now it is more automatic. If I slip, I catch myself much quicker and am then able to put a halt to some of the self-created upset. I am more aware when I get into an unhealthy or unbalanced state and remediate with whatever it is that I need, whether it be rest, exercise, yoga, a focused work period, etc.

Besides my yoga, I now work out on a treadmill or outside walking several times a week and stay on schedule to burn off the frantic energy or alternatively boost my energy to more productive, balanced, Sattva state. I take deliberate breaks to do fun things, and I try to set at least one day each week to come home earlier than usual. I'm trying to be more deliberate in creating opportunities needed to create balance.

Yoga Instruction
My Fourth Hour of Teaching

Wednesday
2/5/14

This hour of teaching was again with my husband Bob and my daughter Catherine, as were my first two hours. This combination is difficult, despite the fact that they are both runners and neither has done much yoga. Cat is very flexible, and my husband is not.

My daughter just turned 16 and throughout her life she has always been involved in one sport or another, including. gymnastics, dance, soccer, kick boxing, and currently she runs cross country and swims. My husband has always been active in sports that have made him strong but tight, including, running, tennis, skiing and sailing.

Years ago, we used to do a great deal of small boat sailing which required a lot of flexibility, but that was before my sixteen-year-old was born. Age has tightened Bob up, too. I found that in the class I taught them, I spent a lot of time propping and modifying Bob, while still trying to challenge Cat. When I did the class with Catherine's friends, I found it much easier as they didn't need many modifications to do a typical sequence. Susie recently commented that teaching gentle yoga was much more challenging than teaching a regular flow class, to which I can now attest.

Working with a person who needs modifications and assistance with alignment is more challenging, but it is teaching me a lot, including learning to listen carefully to and watch my students for signs of stress and to be prepared to teach them a different way, make appropriate modifications, or change my plans for the class. I know from my experience as a teacher in an elementary school that I need to be very flexible based on my student's needs at the time. I also know that it is harder to do that when you do not have the knowledge and experience needed to effortlessly teach the subject whether it is a reading lesson or a yoga class.

Seated Poses and Yoga Nidra

Friday
2/7/2014

Last week, for the first time I started asking myself: "What was I doing in this class". I was tired, less motivated, less excited and a bit intimidated. I asked myself "What am I doing?" "When will I actually have enough time to be able to teach?" and "Am I really cut out to teach yoga?"

Then Susie reminded us that we only had about two months of class left. I couldn't believe it, but instead of making me more motivated, I think I started to feel a little more intimidated and I began thinking "Then what?" One thing I've learned is how much more there is to learn. I was also feeling a bit overwhelmed by my work schedule, class, and my daughter's events (and probably feeling a little guilty, worrying that maybe I wasn't participating enough in her activities).

When I thought about it, I could equate it with the high you get when you first start yoga seriously, which, after a while, is followed by the inevitable lull in motivation. With dedication and persistence in practicing yoga, the positive effects, the motivation and more learning become steadier and satisfying again, but the initial high does not remain. As we've been learning, all feelings, comfortable feelings and uncomfortable ones, are fleeting. They pass, and we return to a state of equilibrium. I also had to remember that the only moments that are real are the ones happening right now; not the ones that may or may not occur in the future.

Instead of dwelling as much on the stress as I may have in the past, I eventually started to tell myself things like, "This feeling will pass.", "It doesn't matter if I ever teach. I've learned and grown so much just being a part of this class.", and "You get out what you put in." I took a break. I slowed down. The break, the knowledge that the feelings would pass, the better attitude, and becoming less attached to the outcome helped me feel more centered.

This week I realized that I could teach somewhere like the YMCA or I could teach friends and family, including the summer project of working with my daughter's cross-country team, but if I don't, that will be OK, too. During the class, I've become more bold with the poses I will try. I've learned more philosophy, I've discovered many more aspects of yoga I want to learn about, I've learned to look for workshops in new places, and I decided to try different studios and types of yoga once this class is done. My energy was returning.

Recently I began writing down balanced sequences for different purposes, including one sequence with no poses that puts weight on the hands (more challenging than it sounds) for a friend who had double mastectomy surgery earlier this year. I am learning; that's for sure. Who knows where any of that will lead?

Tonight, two of our classmates who had been away for two weeks returned to class. They had traveled to India and told us a little about their amazing trip and they bought us each a gift—a change purse handmade by women in India who were trained to do the artwork to become financially independent. It was so nice to have them back.

Class resumed, and we practiced more seated postures. Members of the class taught the poses we learned last week, and Susie went through some new seated poses. Susie is an expert on modifications. She has a gift for seeing what each body needs based on the individual's alignment, facial expressions, and knowledge of anatomy. She gave us many ideas about modifications and poses that shouldn't be done in a larger group because they require individual guidance in order to align them properly and avoid injury, as well as, a warning about over-propping people.

It is important to watch alignment of the spine and choose words carefully, so students are less likely to push themselves into unhealthy positions. Last week Ashley taught us a great way to tell if you are losing the integrity of the spine in a fold. She said to check the area between your pubic bone and your belly button. If your spine is where it should be, that area between the two points will be separated and not squished together. If that area is squished together, it means that your back is curved, and you came forward too far for your body. That made sense to me because I could feel it when I got there. I have to play with the descriptions, though, to make it clearer to a student, because I'm sure Ashley described it more clearly than I did just now.

After all of this, we were treated with Yoga Nidra, which is a guided imagery to lead us to a deep meditative state. As I've said before, I'm not always good with going into a meditative state or activities related to other-people's energy. When we participated in the sound healing for this class, I felt very uncomfortable and I couldn't wait for it to be over.

When I did a Reiki II workshop a couple of years ago, I had a powerful emotional reaction while doing "distance healing" with a classmate in another room. When she felt emotional pain, it appeared that I felt her emotional pain and I just started sobbing for no reason. We weren't in the same room but when I was focused on her, I became upset at the same time she did. Weird, I know. I'm not even sure I believed it, yet there it was.

We also did an "energy" related imagery activity with Nikki, the teacher from Boston, who taught us about yoga philosophy and Thai Yoga Massage, and while others described positive images of their energy field and the energy in the room, I had images of my energy being sucked away as if down a drain leading into the earth. I was left rattled yet again.

So, guided imagery doesn't always go that well for me and I approached this activity open but a little cautious. This time, though, it was different. When we came out of the relaxation state, I actually felt relaxed though very cold, like I did during the sound healing. I don't know if I'm getting better at these activities as I keep trying them, or if it is something else. The Yoga Nidra activity Susie took us through was shorter than the sound healing. That could be the difference, but I also wonder if it was the degree of trust in the leader that made the difference. Perhaps being in a meditative state in a room full of strangers made me feel uncomfortable, while being in a meditative state in a room with a teacher and classmates I've grown fond of and trusted, made me feel safe and comfortable.

I think this issue may be an important consideration if I ever get the opportunity to lead a Yoga Nidra. I will have a better understanding of anyone who doesn't appear to be comfortable during an activity. Again, as with so many sessions I've had during this class, I have more to learn.

Upon reflection, these are amazing activities that suggest humans are more connectable than any of us could have imagined.

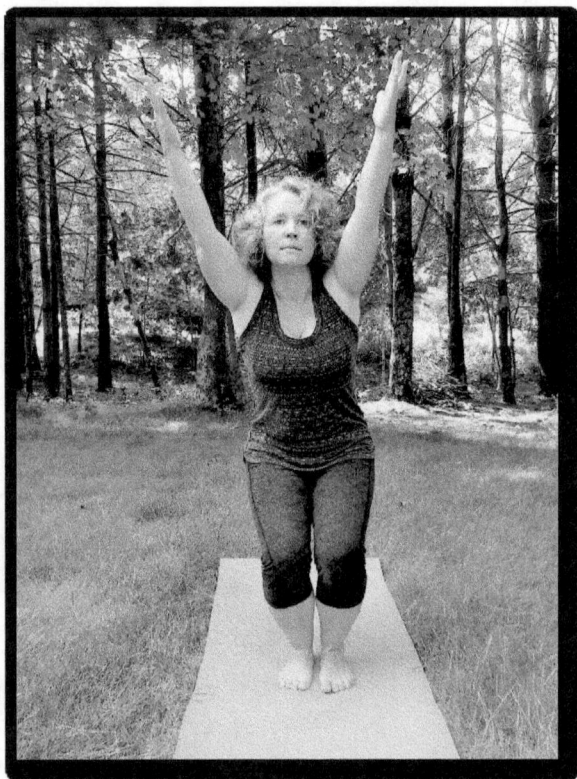

Utkatasana   Chair Pose

Twists, Back Care and Backbends

Weekend
2/14-16/14

This weekend, as with all our weekend trainings, was so full of valuable information that it will take me weeks to process it all! It again humbled me that our instructors know so much, and I know so little, and have so much more to learn about every topic we touched on.

The twists and backbends we learned this weekend will require more practice and study. Some poses we knew well, while others were new or difficult. It was exciting when Susie and Ashley (and some of the class members) assisted students who had never been in a wheel posture before. I will never forget when I got up into wheel the first time with an assist from my first teacher, Allie. In this class, Ashley and Susie used straps under hips and armpits, and the class member coming up in wheel held the ankles of the person assisting at her head.

The wheel posture is a full backbend. It is difficult to describe, but you can see the pose on page 16.

When people got up, I knew exactly how they felt, as I felt that way when Allie helped me up by having me holding her ankles.

After experiencing that, I was able to come into wheel independently. My form needed improvement, but I was up, nonetheless. Once I knew what it was supposed to feel like, which muscles were most engaged, and where the balance was, I was able to get there. When it comes to more difficult poses, I need to feel the pose. Someone can tell me to "spin the inside left hip in", but I can't always get my brain and body to process that right away. Once I feel it though, I can often access it again. This part of the day was exciting. I enjoyed watching people's faces light up as they got into and out of the wheel position, especially those who had some fear going in but tried it anyway. It was beautiful to watch.

On Saturday we spent the day with Liz Owen, who has specialized in yoga for a healthy back. She went through a long sequence and many exercises to strengthen and stretch our abdominal muscles, hip flexors, sacral muscles, and back, to increase back health or ease back problems. I had the idea the sequence would be easy; after all, it was for someone with a bad back and my own back is healthy. However, I found muscles, especially in my abdomen, that I didn't really know were there.

The next day I felt a little sore. That was another lesson in not being attached to preconceived expectations. I learned a tremendous amount and, as always, I have more to learn. Liz has an incredible amount of knowledgeable about anatomy and in how to correct or assist in a variety of complaints and diagnoses, but she also had a gift for teaching. She was patient with us, which was appreciated. Liz and her partner have written a book to share some of her vast knowledge, entitled *Yoga for a Healthy Back*, by Liz Owens and Holly Lebowitz Rossi.

The Business of Yoga & Learning Contentment

Sunday
2/16/2014

Tonight we talked about how to get licensed, how to get insurance, setting pay rates and learning ways to get paid, and jobs. Our group is diverse in their aspirations. Some are already teaching at work, some want to volunteer, some want to begin teaching to get paid, and some, like me, are open to whatever comes, yet are happy just teaching friends and family and deepening our own practice.

I knew that I wouldn't be quitting my day job and jumping full time into teaching, so I was fine with the information given, but I suppose if you thought you were going to be able to make a living as a yoga instructor, the presentation may have been troubling. In our class, we have no one who is starting out in the profession. Many of us are in our thirties, forties, fifties, and older, so we have a lot of responsibilities.

Someone joked that she might be able to quit her stressful, high paying job, and teach yoga. Susie made sure we understood that doing that would not be easy or even wise. The low pay, the lack of jobs and the length of time it takes to build up enough student clientele to make a living are a few of the stumbling blocks to a financially rewarding career. Medical insurance is another issue and then of course you have to find a building or space to rent if you expect to work for yourself.

It is also difficult to get jobs working for a studio unless you are willing to substitute for other teachers when they become unavailable for a lesson. If you specialize in one area of yoga another option is to offer a workshops, as long as you can find a studio that is interested.

Susie, with all of her experience and skill, does teach full time. She works all over Massachusetts driving many miles each day to get to her many studios, classes, and individual clients. She teaches classes in the mornings, afternoons, evenings, and on weekends. That would be a stressful job for me. I'll stick to teaching children in the public school, with a more regular schedule. Susie suggested we teach out of the love of yoga instead of being attached to making a living at it. I am prepared to do that.

Susie also warned that we should not run away from our current circumstances, thinking a major life change will solve our problems. A major life change should be made carefully and thoughtfully and made for the right reasons, based on knowledge and plans. As yogis we can learn to be content despite life's circumstances. I've been working towards that and, as a result, I have found greater satisfaction with my job by focusing in on the aspects that bring me joy, knowing that I provide a valuable learning experience to my students.

I've also been learning to worry less about what others think of me. This is difficult for sure, but with some effort I've learned to let go of my unrealistic expectations and drop some of the negative self-judgment I was prone to harboring. Judith Lasatar in *Living your Yoga* states that expecting more of yourself than others, is a form of egotism because if you think you should do more, then it has to be because you think you are somehow better and should be *able* to do more. That made sense to me. I decided that I didn't need to do more or better than other people after all, and I am much happier for it. I am learning to be honest with myself when I don't meet my goals and have stopped engaging in the negative self-talk.

Being honest allows me to acknowledge that I didn't meet a particular aim ("I didn't do my best", or "I didn't meet a goal"). Self-judgment is assigning negative characteristics to yourself, based on not meeting that aim. ("I am a terrible mother because I was late to the soccer game.")

This goes along with learning to say "no" and standing my ground. I sometimes now say, "Sorry, but I'm not able to do that at this time." These changes took work. Thought processes take effort and don't change themselves, and I do catch myself slipping now and then, but living in the moment allows me to rein it in right away.

These changes, however, have made me much happier in my job, helped me to let go of a lot of old baggage, and have allowed me to show more compassion towards myself and others. For me this yoga teaching course was not an effort to run away, but a chance to enrich what I already had. I understand now that I have amazing opportunities for growth, love, health, and happiness. I'm learning to be grateful for even small moments and everyday simple gifts.

The book "How Yoga Works" by Geshe Michael Roach and Christie McNally illustrates how looking at life circumstances differently helps ease your burdens. Life is difficult by itself, but we can make it even harder or we can make it easier for ourselves. In this book, the authors tell a story to illustrate this point. The main character is a young yogi who finds herself imprisoned, but the story shows how she chose to look at her situation in a unique light and how her view started to change those around her.

So, after finishing our class on the business of yoga, and learning the challenges of earning a living teaching yoga, I am content to use what am learning in the instructor's course to enhance my skills and become a better person and occasionally teach where I am needed.

Yoga Instruction
at the Community Center

Tuesday
2/25/2014

Tonight, I taught at a community center with one of my classmates from the teacher training program. It was a yoga sequence for runners who are training for a half marathon. We are scheduled for second class with this group. I was nervous but focused and we had a great time. We had split the sequence for presenting and, when we weren't teaching, we walked around and gave assists and modifications. At the end people had positive feedback and questions, and the director of programming may ask us back even after our second scheduled class in March. I had fun teaching this group just as much as the groups I have been teaching at home on a less formal basis. After the class I really felt like a teacher. A corner had been turned. One of my classmates described the same feeling after she had completed her practicum sequence. We felt charged and excited.

I'm still excited now as my classmate and I have started to think about, talk about, and plan our next class. This class will be a slower and self-care themed because the athletes in the class will be very close to their half marathon date and they are beginning to feel stressed and burned out from their training.

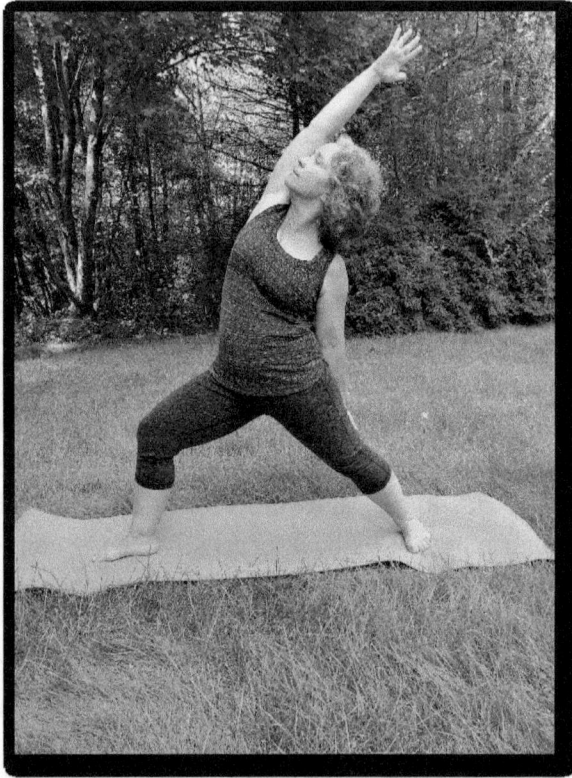

Viparita Virabhadrasana   Reverse Warrior

My Practicum Lesson

Weekend
3/14-6/2014

We have begun our practicum lessons. Because there are 21 of us, and with 35-minute sequences it will take us seven weeks of Fridays to complete them, and that is about what we have left in our teacher training program. I have participated in four of my classmates' lessons and am amazed at the professional level of the classes. The beauty of their readings, their soothing voices, their technical knowledge, the obvious preparedness and the motivating sequences are all so incredible, considering that six months ago most of us had never led a yoga class before. I'm so proud of all of the hard work everyone has done. We have all grown so much and changed while on this journey.

The first sequence of the night was really great, except my classmate used several of the poses I had planned for my presentation. She did them beautifully and of course I was slotted to go next. She and I had coincidently planned the same theme (mindfulness). I chose that because it was one of the most powerful themes I've learned through practicing yoga. It has made my life so much fuller and more at peace, and I wanted to share that. (Despite this, I forgot to practice mindfulness myself tonight!) She did everything so flawlessly that I began to think I should change my sequence on the spot and wing it with something different. I was in a panic mode that I haven't been in for a long time. Yoga is the reason I've been able to dig myself out, but now I'm headed back because of a yoga lesson.

I decided to go on with my planned sequence and let whatever happened, just happen. I started the lesson but was immediately not happy with it. I knew it was a good sequence and I had it under control, but along the way I lost my confidence. I began to go out of the moment and worry about what my classmates would think of it and think of me. That was a big mistake. I attached the outcome of my sequence to what someone else might think, then attached that to who I am. I forgot everything I had been learning for the last three years.

Teaching this sequence was so much harder than teaching my teenagers or even the session at the community center. First, I cared too much about what my classmates and teachers would think. Second, I started comparing my work to that of others, and my own judgments started beating me up. *Attachment.* I saw a glimpse of someone I had hoped was gone, an old self I thought I had left behind. At least I recognized the unhealthy thought pattern sooner than later and was able to move on, but not before my practicum had ended.

I held some of the poses in my sequence too long, got off my timing (despite all of the practice that made me think I could be on target), messed up several lefts and rights, stumbled on some key points and made too many points (which messed my timing up even more), lost my place once and had to very obviously move people back into a completely different position. I needed to decide on the spot which poses I should drop to get back on track. My music started out too loud and I had to lower it. That was the easiest mistake to fix (and I was complimented on noticing the problem and repairing it quickly and without drawing attention to it.). I continued on my error bound journey and made the class laugh in order to move on from my mistakes. People liked that. I think I was being mindful to some degree during the lesson, as evidenced by some of my split-second changes and being able to move on with a sense of humor.

After the lesson was over, however, I let myself leave the moment to allow myself to be harsh and unkind as I rehashed the sequence in my head, instead of looking at what could be learned and moving on. The problems in the sequence will be corrected with experience and practice. The attachment issue was what caused me suffering after it was over. I had pictured a perfect sequence; therefore, I made myself suffer when I didn't live up to my unrealistic expectations. Instead, I fell into self-judgment instead of loving kindness.

When it was time for feedback, I braced myself, but it was good, overall. Suggestions for improvement included: timing, left/rights, and being sure to use positive wording (for what I need to see, not what I don't want to see). I'm sure I will process the rest as I settle my mind. Things people liked included the fact that I made people feel at ease and that they had fun, and some liked the flow of the class. I actually heard a lot of compliments along with suggestions. Some people seemed surprised that I could pull a teacher voice out of my usual soft-spoken voice. One person said it helped her have more confidence that she will be able to do that when her turn to teach comes. One classmate said that the way I handled the bigger mistake in my sequence helped her to feel more confident in knowing she could handle it if she made a mistake in a class. I kept thinking to myself, what kind people they were. 'Why were they being so nice?' I was so disappointed with myself, and my friends were telling me that I did well.

So now I needed to detach and think about the lessons more realistically but kindly. I made mistakes and it was Ok. The sky didn't fall, and my class did not abandon me. They seemed to enjoy my presentation and now that it is over, I am fine. If they didn't enjoy the class, it would still be over, and I would still be fine. I will teach again. Things will go right, and things will go wrong. Neither outcome means I am good or bad; just human. People think and feel differently and all we can do is our best. Prepare and work hard but try not to be attached to the outcome. Let the difficult emotions come in and let them go out. Don't attach to either. Breathe.

Some things I will do differently to prepare for my next class are: 1. Do more research on the benefits and contraindications of the poses I'm doing (I really liked that in one of my classmate's sequences.); 2. Make sure I have planned places to cut or plan simpler sequences as needed; 3. Figure out a way to keep my rights and lefts straight; and 4. Find a place and make time to center myself before beginning. This will come with time, practice, experience and continued learning.

Then it was over.

The good news is that I am done with *my* practicum sequence...inhale, exhale. The bad news is that I am done with my practicum sequence…screech, whine, cry. I worked hard on my sequence to make sure it touched every part of the body and that it had adequate warm up, peak poses, and a cool down. I learned to teach a breathing technique that was new for me - "Nadi Shodanna", alternate nostril breathing, which I find centering. I have been learning and struggling at times with meditative practices and breath-work, and as a leap of faith I decided to include the breathing technique in my sequence as a personal challenge to extend myself, and that went well.

I practiced the sequence over and over, taught it in a class with neighbors, timed it with music, and looked up the poses online for positioning and alignment points and Sanskrit names. I repeatedly watched videos and read *Yoga Journal* write ups of the breathing technique and some of the poses. In the end, some parts went well, while some parts needed improvement. I have learned from the experience and am better for it. Sometimes things don't go exactly according to plan, but that is OK. Breathe, learn, grow, and move on

.

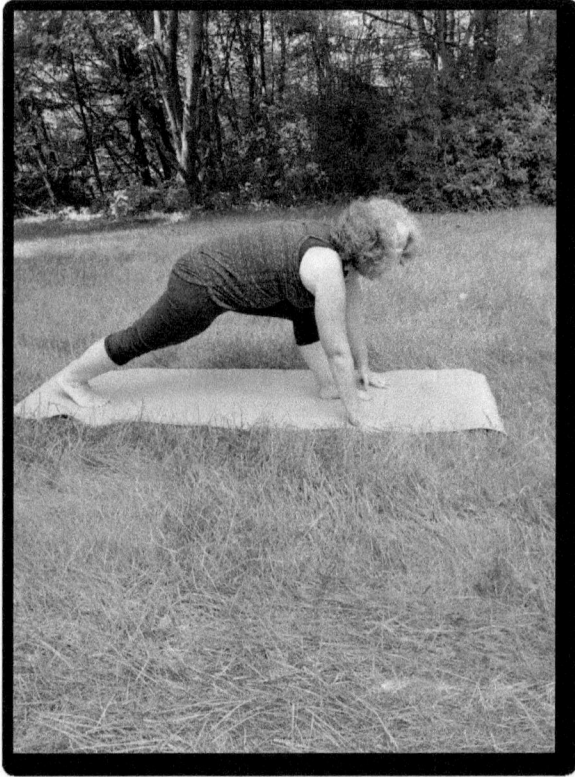

Utthita Ashwa Sanchalanasana   Lunge Pose

Anatomy with Chanel Luck

Saturday
3/15/2014

This weekend, we had another amazing experience. Thank you, Ashley and Susie. Chanel Luck spent the weekend teaching us anatomy and how it directly related to yoga poses. Her teaching was so clear, and she was able to take us from where we were. The anatomy book we were using in class was difficult for me as a beginner, but this instruction helped make sense out of all of the information. The teaching was so connected to yoga practice and focused on the people who might find themselves in our classes.

There is much too much to share completely about this weekend training, but there were two main lessons that Chanel wove through everything we did. They were: 1. "A little anatomy goes a long way!"; and 2. Every person who walks through the doors to our classes is unique, has unique needs, and an accurate assessment of needs is required to give each person appropriate cues to meet individual needs.

There is no cookie cutter model for cues to fit people; even those with similar diagnoses. This circled back to a conversation I had early on with my husband, Bob, when I began trying out my first sequence on him. He asked, "Who is this sequence aimed at?" The answer should always be: "The sequence is aimed at the individual needs of the students who attend the class."

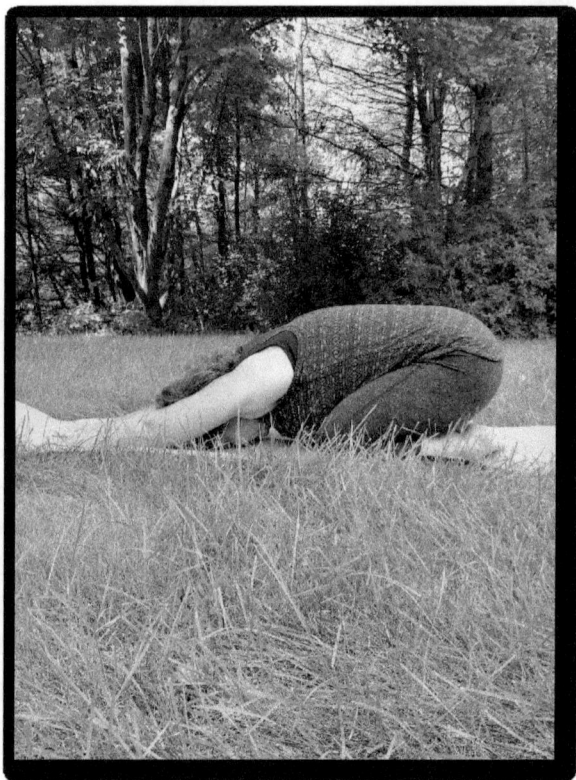

Utthita Balasana   Extended Child's Pose

Family

Friday
3/21/2014

Tonight, yet again, the people in my class who presented their practicum classes used their individual strengths to make unique and beautiful sequences. It was wonderful, as all of the classes have been to date. We're all at different stages and have different needs, but we're working hard and developing our skills and knowledge. I am again amazed by how much we have learned and by how much we have changed.

The experience we have had has touched each of us greatly. I think of Nikki, one of our guest teachers, who described the experience and learning as creating a crevasse that will make space for a trickle of more learning and life changes. For each of us, what we do with this course and what the learning will do for us will be different and may change at different times. It could be a trickle or an ocean, but we have all been touched.

A powerful thought came over me tonight as I realized what else we have gained from this experience. I looked around at all the faces as we gave feedback for each of the teachers presenting tonight. The feedback was very thoughtful and individual, based on what we knew about the person. Because we have spent so much time learning and growing together, we know what each member of the group needs to hear, what their strengths have been, and which aspects they each have been working on the most. We talked about their focuses and struggles and their victories, based on where they began.

As I looked at those giving feedback, I also realized that I know as much or more about these people as I do some people I've worked with for years. We know simple things, like who lives on a farm and who has small children. We know who has a new job and who teaches or participates in other physical activities, such as running marathons, teaching spin classes and Pilates, and playing hockey. We know who has osteoporosis, scoliosis, back problems, food allergies, food preferences, and previous surgeries.

As a result of this experience, we have become a family. I think we might be treating each other even better than some biological families treat each other. We have striven to support each other and we show caring and encouragement through all of the work and growth we have been doing. I don't think anyone saw any of our work as a competition. We have been happy and sad for each other through different circumstances. Life is ever-changing, and "this too will pass", as they say, but some of the friendships and connections made here will be lasting.

The experience of meeting and growing with so many wonderful, unique and caring people is something I will always carry with me, regardless of any other future outcomes.

Yoga Instruction
Going Solo at the Community Center
More about Mindfulness and Attachment

Wednesday
3/26/2014

Today was one of those days. I've been coming back from a nasty stomach bug, so I didn't feel fabulous. At work we had several big projects and parents, children, and school personal requests were constant with unexpected demands for miracles, some of which I was able to pull off, but others weren't even close. It seemed like every time I had a plan or strategy to turn the day around, something else popped up to block it. I felt I couldn't do anything I was supposed to do well in this day of constant chaos.

Again, can you guess what caused the negative feelings? Problem one was the attachment to my plans for the day, difficulty adapting to the new and changed plans, and the attachment to being seen as capable by the people making requests of me all day. Problem two was the fact that if I were being more mindful and tackling one problem at a time, it would have felt much different. I did succeed in bringing myself back as my mind wandered off to what I had to have done in the future so I could get back to the present and get done what needed to be done now based on my priorities.

To make this work, you have to keep asking yourself: "What has to be done right now?" and let go of the rest for the moment. I did handle the day pretty well over all. I wasn't beating myself up, which was a good thing, but I was still extremely cranky, and I just wanted to go home and go to bed. By the time I slinked out the door, I felt drained and empty.

"So," you may ask, "What has this all got to do with the Community Center Yoga Class I was teaching?" Well, this was the night I was taking on that class without my teaching partner. I knew I had to do something to recharge and let go of the negativity to be effective and helpful to the students coming to the yoga class that evening.

First, I came home and saw my husband and daughter for a few minutes before they headed out to one of her activities. After that, I blasted some music, I washed up, changed and had a small snack. Next, I forced myself into some quiet time to do some alternate nostril breathing. Ok; so far so good. I was calmer, but still exhausted. I headed for the community center. I got there about 45 minutes early and made sure I had everything set up and organized.

Last week, one of my classmates set up two mats in a T at the front so it was easy to demo from the front or side. I opted to try that, and it worked well. Everything was set and, although my nerves gave me a little lift, I was still exhausted. More importantly, I still felt empty.

What I did next saved the evening. I decided since I was already set up why not have my own practice before the class? This could even make up for my lost practice time since I've been in the teacher training mode. That is, my practice lately has been more focused on teaching, or what Susie calls practicing with a teacher's mind instead of a student's mind, which is totally different. I thought: "Taking a few minutes of personal practice time couldn't make my class any worse and who knows; it could even help." It wasn't really so much of a thought as just the whisper of a need.

So, there I was. I just started practicing—not reviewing my class sequence or reviewing my focus; just practicing from the heart. That is when I started getting my energy back and I started to feel like myself again. Although I was expending some energy, I was also recharging and creating more energy.

By the time the students arrived, I felt relaxed, present, focused and ready to be the teacher. I had lived the lesson Susie and Ashley had been teaching us since day one, which is to be loving to yourself and to continue with your own practice, so you will have what you need to give back to others. After giving myself some self-love, I was better able to move on and detach completely from the earlier part of the day.

With a planned focus on love and kindness to self, the class went well. People seemed satisfied at the end and had positive feedback. The class was much smaller than last time, with only six students, and the gentle practice with a slow pace gave me more time to peek at notes (Great advice about child's pose. Thanks Ashley!).

When the lesson was over, during my self-assessment, a weakness jumped out at me. I still have difficulty mirroring and correctly calling rights and lefts when the poses get more complicated (put your right hand on your left knee and your left hand, etc.). This didn't bother the class as much as it bothered me.

First, I did use the trick Susie and Ashley suggested of just saying to "take the opposite hand to the opposite knee…" I also realized that in lateral poses, it is possible to use descriptors that involved the front and back limb. (Yes, Susie and Ashley probably told us that, too, but I guess I needed more practice to internalize it.) Later in the class, when walking around the students to check posture (which is frightening at first but was OK in my slower, gentler class), I could be behind the students facing in the same direction, which made giving right-left directions much easier.

Of course, not being in the front of the class facing the students only works when you don't have to demonstrate a move, but it is one more trick in the bag to be used in a pinch. I expect I'll get better at the mirroring an entire class and will discover additional strategies with more opportunities to teach.

At the end of my presentation, I read a quote from Rolf Gates (*Meditations from the Mat*, p. 23), in which he said, "Love is not a thought. It is an action. And each loving action that we take infuses us with more energy for loving action in the future." I'm glad I decided to apply that to myself before I tried to read it to my students. When I practiced this, I realized how powerful it is.

Fast Forward Four Years

Here is the good news: I have improved significantly and I have a great deal more confidence when teaching and mirroring. Practice is what increased my skill. One thing I did that helped for a while when I began teaching was putting a red hair elastic on my left wrist to remind me that when I was mirroring, my left was their right (red/right). I used that for months, but soon I discovered that I didn't need it and it became more automatic.

I still make a mistake now and then, (as do teachers I take classes with). The difference is I just correct it and move on. If I don't make a big deal about it, the class doesn't either, which is exactly what Susie said would happen when I was so worried about it.

Another fact is that when I'm not worrying about it I can think more clearly and make fewer mistakes. I also need to remind myself that I am the only one in the room who knows the intended sequence so if I mess up, who would know?

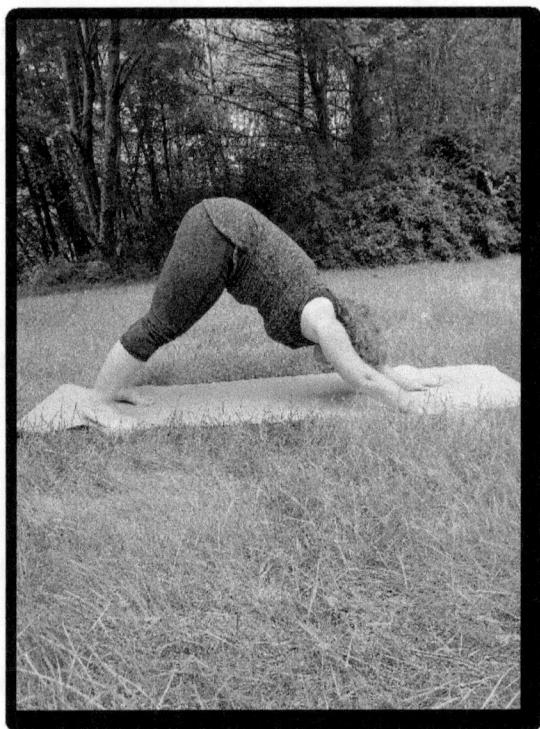

Adho Mukha Svanasana
Downward-Facing Dog

Panic During Yoga

Friday
3/28/2014

Tonight, was to be another incredible evening of practices. We had three great classes, including a heart chakra sequence, chanting by candle light, and a guided imagery practice. Each week, I am overwhelmed by the uniqueness of my classmates' presentations. The program was spiritually focused, and I was looking forward to three hours of relaxed enlightenment, contentment and bliss until the unexpected happened.

The first sequence started with an intense breathing activity (*Pranayama*). We breathed in and out repeatedly with increasing speed, pushing the breath out with our abdominal muscles. I soon began to feel lightheaded and then a sensation that I couldn't breathe. My heart started racing and I began to gasp for air. I knew immediately I was going into a panic attack, which I have experienced before in times of stress.

Full blown panic attacks are terrifying and can be debilitating. They involve extreme feelings of fear accompanied with a long list of physical responses including rapid heart rate, shortness of breath, tightness in throat and chest pain, for example.

Yoga has been a godsend for me and the three years of practice, before I took the instructor's class, has saved me from experiencing these extreme symptoms of anxiety and panic attacks; so, having these symptoms triggered by a yoga exercise was unsettling to say the least. My go-to has gone away.

I resisted the urge to leave the room and began talking myself down, breathing slowly and working my way through the rest of the yoga lesson. The classmate who was teaching has a lovely soothing voice, and the sequence had a unique spiritual focus. There were heart opening poses later in the sequence that helped ease some of my symptoms.

Upon reflection I realized I was also upset with myself for having this panic reaction which only added to my discomfort.

During the feedback period I told the class what happened. I was embarrassed, but our class community was a safe place and we were all there to learn and to support each other. I found that my experience wasn't completely unique and the discussion became a teaching moment for everyone.

The message? First, teaching and practicing deep-breathing exercises is one of the Eight Limbs, an important part of yoga that provides significant benefits including: increased oxygen supply to the body, calming of the nerves, muscle relaxation, lowering blood pressure, strengthening the heart and lungs and increased ability to focus and concentrate.

Second, when teaching breathing activities, articulate clearly to the class that if it doesn't feel right, slow the breath and go back to normal breathing. Dizziness and tingling sensations are not uncommon, and although anxiety over the exercise and panic are far less common, the teacher needs to be attentive to their students' reactions to forestall such an event.

After the feedback, Susie put me in child's pose (*balasana*) and lay on top of me, back to back, to slow my nervous system and get me grounded. I could feel my heartbeat slow and started to feel better. I stayed down in the child pose for a few more breaths then took a break in another room with one of my classmates. By the time the next student began her yoga lesson I felt well enough to continue the class even though the tightening in my neck and back had not completely gone away.

Fast Forward Four Years

I have not had a panic attack during any yoga activity since that class and, in fact, have not had a panic attack anywhere in any situation since that time. Learning to feel feelings, recognize stress (physical and emotional) and tailoring my yoga practice to meet my needs continues to keep me healthy and centered. The key is recognizing and addressing your needs.

As for students in the yoga classes I teach, I am on the lookout for signs of stress and discomfort of any kind and specifically for a halt or change in breathing, facial expressions, and favoring one body part. Being aware of these symptoms helps me give feedback, adjust positions, or suggest modifications. The lesson is to observe your students and respond to their needs. Where have you heard that before?

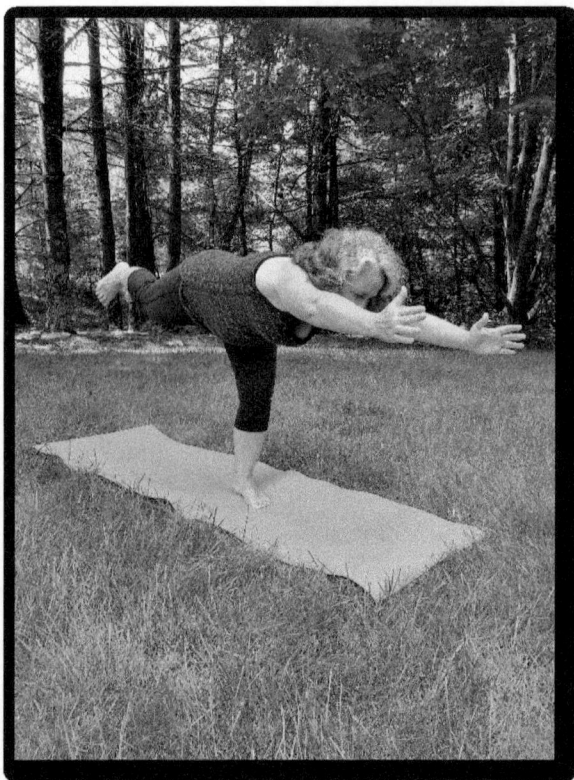

Virabhadrasana III   Warrior III

Kundalini Yoga

Weekend
4/11-13/2014

The week before this session I was a bit apprehensive. I understood *Kundalini* yoga to be a very spiritual practice including chanting, breath work, and meditation. After having a problem with more advanced breath work last week, I wasn't sure about participating in another session that might include the same kind of breath work so soon. I decided to go early and sit in the back so that if I couldn't participate I would be near the door if I needed to leave.

As it turned out, I learned a great deal and enjoyed the experience. I'm still not sure *Kundalini* is the practice for me, but I loved certain aspects of what I learned, and I will be exploring some of the chanting and prayers that we covered in class. The purpose of this practice is to uplift people and tap into the inner spirit, one premise being that people need to be uplifted to deal with adversity and to feel hope and love.

The teacher, Kate, who presented this class, was lovely. She was another teacher who radiated a kind, peaceful presence. Because she was modeling a traditional *Kundalini* for us, she wore all white, including a white turban covering her hair.

Kundalini teachers dress in white and follow prescribed sequences or sets chosen from a book, developed by Yogi Bhajan.

The teacher is likely to have a book of the prescribed sets visible, as well as a timer. The sequences follow a strict pattern, starting with a chant or mantra, moving to warm ups, then moving to timed sets or sequences, and they close with an Irish folk song. We did a short sequence. The chanting was beautiful. I've had little exposure to this practice, but thanks to my classmates' practicums (which included chanting), some of the guest teachers who began with chants, and this class on Kundalini that included chanting, I have become more comfortable with it.

I've decided that, in addition to breathing and breath awareness exercises, some chanting could encourage mindfulness and relaxation, especially if the words or the translations of the words resonate with the person chanting them. I've already downloaded a couple of the chants I liked into my iPod. My two favorites at this time are "Lokah Samastha (slow version)" by Sharon Gannon and "Guru Ram Das" by Guru Ganesha Singh.

The sequence we followed was unusual, but I was relieved to note that it did not include any breathing techniques that required holding or withholding breath, so I stayed for the entire class. I'm glad I had the exposure and I can decide if I'd like to explore this type of yoga further.

Ayurveda

Saturday
4/12/2014

Kate, our teacher for *Kundalini*, returned the next day to teach us about *Ayurveda* principles. She considered Ayurveda the "sister science" to yoga. It focuses on caring for the body, mind, and spirit. If you would like to be evaluated by someone who is trained in Ayurveda, you will be given recommendations related to your diet, sleep needs, yoga poses, mantras, etc. that are best for your constitution. A person's constitution is based on the *Dochas*.

In an earlier class with Susie, we learned about the three *Gunas* (*Satvic*, meaning balanced; *Rajasic*, meaning fiery/energized; and *Tamasic*, meaning sluggish/heavy). These are qualities of people, foods, and things around us.

The three *Doshas* pertain to the imbalances we all tend towards. These types of imbalances aren't by themselves good or bad, as all three have characteristics that are desirable and challenging. The **Vatta** constitution is related to wind, air, or ether. A person with this propensity may be mobile, funny, light, less confrontational, and out there in the world. The ***Pitta*** constitution is associated with fire, water, and oil. A person with this propensity may be active, hardworking, inspiring, and driven. The **Kapha** constitution is associated with earth, water, and oil. A person with this propensity may be dependable, solid, nurturing, and likely to be a homebody. Each of these Dochas has typical physical characteristics as well as personality characteristics, and they each have recommendations to follow for better health and balance.

Based on physical description and other characteristics, I appear to be a *Kapha/Pitta* or a *Kapha/Vatta*. I'm not really sure. I believe I live with two Pitta personalities (my husband and daughter). I'll have to find out more about what that means for health and balance according to Ayurveda medicine.

Kate gave some universal recommendations that are believed to help everyone. These are: scraping the tongue (apparently you can get a tongue scraper at a health food store or use a spoon), drinking a cup of hot water in the morning before eating anything to stimulate digestion, giving yourself a self-massage with oil before your shower, cooking with turmeric, and using a neti pot. It is possible to take workshops, have a professional evaluate your constitution, and get books on the topic of Ayurveda to find out more. Kate recommended a book called "Ayurveda for Women", by Dr. Robert E. Svoboda.

Journey's End or Beginning?
Graduation

Monday
4/28/2014

Susie and Ashley were incredible teachers and mentors by themselves, but they also brought in other amazing people and experiences to help us become well rounded and informed. We were blessed during our 200-hour instructors' course due in part to the incredible connections Susie and Ashley have with so many talented yoga teachers from Boston and surrounding areas that came into our class to offer their knowledge and wisdom. But now it is over.

Tonight, my classmates and I received our certificates for completing our 200-hour yoga teacher certification course! We all brought food and shared our evening together to celebrate our accomplishment. We were excited to receive our certificates, but there was definitely a downside to the celebration as we understood that everything was changing. For the last seven months we spent nearly every Friday night learning and practicing yoga, as well as attending seven weekend workshops. That is a lot of time together. In an earlier entry I noted how close we had become and now, as everything does, our relationships will again change somehow.

Don't get me wrong; I will be glad to have a free Friday night, but we will miss our time and learning together. At the party someone noted that since we came from such different walks of life it would have been unlikely we would have ever met if not for this class.

We have several homemakers, people working in finance, teachers, nurses, an EMT, a Pilates instructor, a doctor, a masseuse, a professional flute player, and an occupational therapist, to name a few. We were from all over Mass, RI, and even New Hampshire. Despite this, our original intentions were similar, even if we didn't know where the class would lead. We did know that we wanted to learn more about yoga and be able to improve our own experience and somehow share what we learned with others.

Some of my classmates are already teaching their own classes or substitute teaching. Maybe some still don't know where this will lead—like me. I have started to register with Yoga Alliance. As soon as they get a confirmation from the studio that I completed the course, they will email me with the next steps and I'll be able to sign up for insurance and move on. Many possibilities have crossed my mind and I am looking forward.

I've signed up for a two-day workshop on assisting, which will allow me to volunteer to assist an experienced teacher with classes. This also means I'll already have some hours to count towards my next certification in three years.

Co-workers have asked if I could teach a class after school. I'm not sure if the school department would allow that, but it is one possibility. Interestingly, I've also thought about volunteering at a local nursing home. In addition, I've considered contacting my local YMCA to see if they might want someone to do a beginner's class or series.

I've ordered two books about children's yoga that Ashley recommended, as I am reconsidering teaching that age level. (The books are "Planting Seeds" by Thich Nhat Hanh and "Plum Village Community" and "Yoga Calm for Children" by Lynea Gillen, MS and Jim Gillen, RYT.) When we had the workshop on children's yoga I initially thought I would not like to do that for many reasons, but I don't want to completely close the door on the possibility.

There was a comfort level in expecting to teach what I was most familiar with. With this course, though, I've gained enough knowledge to explore other forms of yoga. With children's yoga, I can take what I know about children and combine that with what I know about yoga for a good match. I'm not sure how, when or where that could play out. Perhaps it will happen by adding more components when possible to my students' school day. In the end, of course, I'll be teaching a form of yoga that is best for and meets the needs of my students.

I've discovered that I will not likely be teaching the style of yoga I practice right away, and that is alright. I've gained confidence and I realize now that I can teach a variety of types of classes that don't match the mixed-level Vinyasa classes I have typically taken. Susie and Ashley gave us so much incredible instruction and at least an introduction to so many different topics, including children's yoga, chair yoga, and yoga in pregnancy (not to teach a prenatal class, but enough to take care of a person coming into a class who happens to be pregnant), as well as a background in proper alignment, anatomy, assists, etc.

Although I still have what feels like a world of information to learn about each of those types of classes and topics, I have a base to begin with. At this point, I believe it would be more likely for me to be teaching a beginners' class or volunteering somewhere. Given that I am a beginning teacher, and since I work full time and have a family, my schedule may not allow the subbing required to gain needed experience at a studio. During the school year, I realistically couldn't teach more than once a week. Volunteering or teaching a series of classes would be more attainable.

As you can see, I have few firm plans, but I am trying to be open to opportunities that might come along. The future is full of changes and possibilities, and I've learned to make an effort to be open to new things. I think the journey has begun anew as much as it has ended.

Before I close this chapter, I would like to extend my immeasurable gratitude to my teachers, Susie and Ashley at "The State of Grace Yoga and Wellness Center", as well as to Nancy, the owner of "State of Grace". I would also like to thank all of my wonderful classmates for their love, support and kindness, and for all they each have taught me. I feel blessed that you have all crossed my path.

"May the longtime sun shine upon you, all love surround you, and the pure light within you, guide your way on." - Irish Folk Song

Namaste!

Fast Forward Four Years

Journey's End or Beginning?

Like my classmates, I became aware that the end of our class was the beginning of a change in our lives. When I first completed this course, I participated in a few more workshops in assists at a local studio, yoga for anxiety and depression (with Bo Forbes), and other topics before I started teaching.

Eventually I began offering yoga class sessions six weeks at a time at my school for other teachers. I have also occasionally taught at a community project in the summer for an organization conceived and fostered by some of my teacher training peers. The Sunshine Yoga Collaborative set out to help offer yoga to the community in Uxbridge, MA, for a small donation that would go to a community charity. On one occasion, I taught a few private classes for a friend, which was the only time (so far) that I have been paid for teaching yoga. I am now considering trying a children's class.

With a full-time job and other responsibilities, I haven't felt I could commit to a paid class schedule, but as I have been learning, it is impossible to know what lies ahead if you are open to new experiences. Many of my teacher training peers do teach professionally. Others volunteer to teach classes as I do. At least one did leave a well-paying job to explore a career in yoga. I see some of my classmates regularly, I see some on occasion, and I have lost touch with others. Regardless, they will always hold a place in my heart.

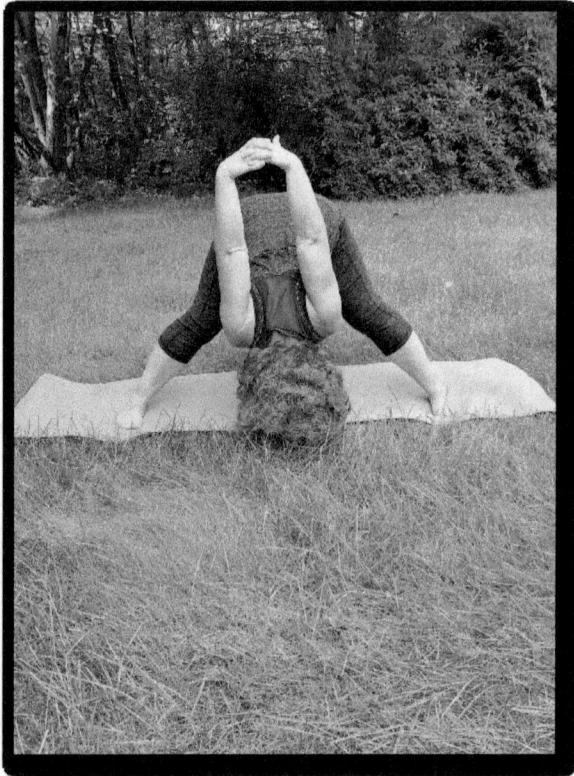

Prasarita Padottanasana
Wide-Legged Standing Forward Fold

Lessons I Have Learned

Here are the primary lessons I have learned through taking the 200-hour yoga instructor's course, practicing yoga for myself, teaching yoga to others and digging deep into my soul.

1   Yoga (*yuj*) is based on a south Asian 7000-year-old culture that is foreign to our western world. The practice of yoga (*asanas*, *pranayama* and meditation) then requires a change in mindset, a leap of faith and a lot of work.

2   Let experiences, feelings in, then let them pass through you and then leave, like fleeting clouds in the sky.

3   By eliminating the worry about the past and the future you are able to do more and to live more fully in the moment.

4   Be open to changes in life, situations, and to yourself. Don't define yourself or your life so strictly that you don't allow room for growth.

5   If you can let go of your expectations and attachment to outcomes, you will be able to better appreciate, experience and enjoy your time in the moment.

6   By living in the moment, my emotions are connected to reality, not separate from it. I have found this to be a life altering approach to living that has dramatically reduced my anxiety and improved the quality of my life.

7   I cannot control others or events and trying to do so will only cause me misery. But I can control what I do, and with effort and insight, I can control what I think and feel.

8   I can be a good influence on others and contribute to positive outcomes by being true to myself and knowing that my words and my behavior have an effect on others.

9   All feelings, comfortable and uncomfortable, are fleeting and will eventually change, because they are based on perceptions that are unique to you. Strong emotions that come from rumination are not based on reality and will lead us astray.

10   Negative feelings are created when we attach our self-esteem to the opinions of others. We can prevent this from happening by basing our self esteem on realistic expectations for our own thoughts and behaviors.

11 Putting off tasks creates anxiety from the burden of knowing that you have unfinished business and the time lost spent thinking about what you have to do.

12   We need to show compassion and kindness to ourselves first. If we don't take care of ourselves, we will not have the strength, patience, and love to act compassionately toward others.

13   To be truly compassionate we must be able is to see our connection to others. When we see this connection, we are better able to understand that we could find ourselves in the other person's circumstances and he or she in ours.

14   Compassion is: 1 Knowing where someone is at a given time, 2 Understanding what it took for them to get there, and 3 Not helping them unless they ask you to.

15   Every yoga student has a unique emotional and physical level that requires ongoing assessment by the instructor that may require modifications or even lesson-revisions by the teacher.

16   A yoga teacher's first responsibility is to be aware of the student's ability and limitations while teaching and be willing to adjust the lesson to their needs and levels and not blindly follow a lesson plan for the sake of the plan itself.

17   When teaching yoga, you can't give more than you have, so you need to practice yoga for yourself to grow and increase what you do have to give others.

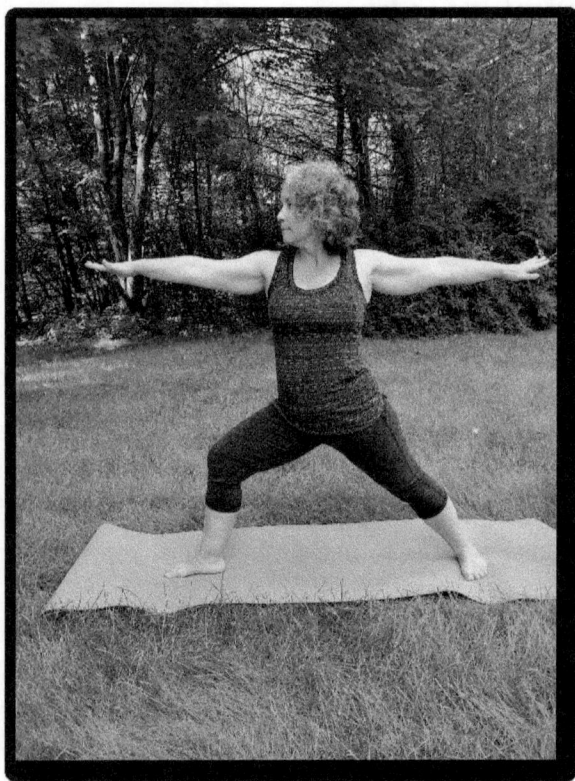

Virabhadrasana II   Warrior II

Elementary Teacher Resources

In addition to being a certified yoga instructor, I am also a second grade teacher in Rhode Island and since my training, I've used yoga in the classroom to help my students calm their mind, increase their focus, and become aware of their body in space and of others around them.

The essence of yoga is to learn to "know thyself," and gain a broader perspective on what to take in and what to let go. I try to help my little ones know they have power to help themselves. One of my little guys told me with a smile, "I was very excited and nervous, and I took some deep breaths and now I feel calmer." What more could I ask of this child? Here are three activities I incorporate into my second-grade class. You can download idea cards and more information for free from my website:

www.yogawithlisa.org. Then go to "Teacher Resources."

1. Mindfulness Yoga Exercise

Begin and end yoga poses and movement breaks with breathing exercises. Ask the children to think about how they are feeling physically and otherwise. Sometimes I'll ask for a group response like a thumbs up and down, or say something like, "Wiggle your fingers if you feel...?" The goal is to get them to become more aware of their feelings and body sensations that give them clues about what they need during the day. This should be a quick check-in of the body and mind, and children should eventually learn to do this independently. The more children become attuned to their emotional and physical wellbeing, the easier it will be for them to make minor adjustments or "head off" deeper feelings that could create behavior and emotional problems later on.

2. Children's Breathing Exercises

Deep breathing will bring you back to the moment. I teach my students several breathing techniques and explain that these can help us calm and focus our bodies and minds, bringing us back to the present moment. After teaching the breathing techniques, I periodically see individual students in the class using one of the breaths during the day. Children do learn to respond to their sensations. **Download** from my website Mindfulness and Deep-Breathing Yoga Exercise description card and the Deep-Breathing Sequence cards.

3. Classroom Movement Breaks

Movement breaks give children a chance to be in their bodies, notice how they feel, and discharge a little extra energy or stress. They are also fun. These breaks involve short yoga sequences or games.

I do some yoga moves with the breaks involving a sequence of poses, but I also incorporate dancing, the hokey pokey, the twist, disco moves, or cross body moves that are good for brain development (like touching your left elbow to your right knee). This year I tried a game from Lisa Flynn's workshop which involves standing in star pose and singing "Twinkle Little Star" while rocking from one foot to the other. The children love it! Another game that is usually a crowd favorite is a version of musical chairs involving dancing while the music plays and freezing instead of sitting when the music stops. I typically end movement breaks with "being a statue" to allow the children to be a little creative while also hitting the pause and knowing the sequence is coming to an end. I say, "Remember; statues don't move or talk...". Deep breathing is another alternative or additional end to movement breaks. **Download** from my website the Movement-Breaks Description and the Movement -Breaks Sequence cards.

These activities are short but effective. There isn't enough time in a school day and activities added should not take away from other learning. The activities should make academic learning easier by helping students to refocus, calm down, and move to the next important learning activity. Some activities can also be integrated with other learning, including social skills instruction, snack time, or morning meetings. I am continuing to try new things with my students and, as in all areas of my yogic journey, I am learning new things every day.

Tadasana   Mountain Pose

142

Choosing a Yoga Studio

Learning yoga is an individual and complex journey. You need to explore why you want to practice yoga and why you would want to take a teacher training program and decide generally what you want to get out of taking the course. Remember that both will evolve as you learn and grow.

Practicing yoga daily or a few times each week will help you tease out your needs and what you expect to gain. Practice can include physical poses (asanas), breathing, reading, reflecting, meditation, etc. Read daily and take notes. Try yoga at different studios or online. Experiment with different styles. See what type of yoga resonates with you.

Not every yoga studio offers the 200-hour instructor's course, which means you may have to begin a fresh search for one that does. Begin by attending a few yoga sessions, which will give the opportunity to talk to students and staff and assess how comfortable you feel in the studio.

Here are a few questions that are worth answering.

- Is the studio reputable?
- Is the teacher reputable?
- Is the program certified by Yoga Alliance?
- Does the physical environment see comfortable?
- Does the time frame give you enough time to complete all the requirements and process what you've learned?

- What type of yoga are you most interested in?
- Can you meet the teacher before choosing and ask him/her questions?
- Do you feel comfortable with this teacher?

Searching for a good program and, even more importantly, finding a program that is good for you, takes patience, time and thought. Be sure you have completed your research and are pleased with your results before you register.

Good Luck.

Coming to Terms

The original language of yoga was written in Sanskrit, the classical language of India and Hinduism 7000 - 8000 years ago predating Greek and Latin. Each of the 50 letters (A-Y) when spoken with the proper sound frequency are designed to provide a therapeutic benefit which offers a double benefit when connecting a yoga pose with its Sanskrit name.

Eight Limbs Path <u>page 25</u>

1 **Yamas** Five Moral Restraints
   Satya: truthfulness
   Asteya: non-stealing
   Brahmacarya: moderation
   Aparigraha : non-hoarding

2 **Niyamas** Five Observances
   Sauca : purity
   Santosa : contentment
   Tapas: austerity
   Svadhyaya : self-study
   Isvara-pranidhana: devotion to a higher power

3 **Asanasa** yoga poses

4 *Pranayama* Focused Breathing

5 *Pratyahara* turning inward

6 *Dharana* concentration

7 *Dhyana* meditation

8 Samadhi union of self

Surya Namaskar Sun Salutation sequence   page 34
  Tadasana Mountain Pose
  Pranamasana Prayer Pose
  Urdhva Hastasana Upward Salute
  Uttanasana Forward Fold
  Ardha Uttanasana flat back
  Anjaneyasana Low Lunge
  Uttihita Chaturanga Dandasana High Plank
  Chaturanga Dandasana come to the floor
  Urdhva Mukha Svanasana Upward Facing Dog
  Adho Mukha Svanasana Downward Facing Dog

Dharma   page 45
  A way of life, cosmic order, Buddha teachings

Sanskrit Man page 69
Garudasana Garuda:eagle *Asana*:pose
Janu Sirsasana   Janu:knee, Sirsa:head, *Asana*:pose
Navasana Nava:boat *asana*:pose
Tadasana Urdhva Hastasana
          Urdva:upward, *Hasta*:hand/arm, *Asana*:pose

Gunas Three States page 81
  Rajas: associated with fire, passion, high activity, and heat.
  Tama: state in which people appear to be idle, tend towards
darkness or dullness
  Sattva: associated with a lightness of being, serenity, and a
feeling of well-being

Kapalabhati passive and forceful breathing   page 84

Parivrkta Uktinasana revolved chair   page 84

Gomukhasan cow face pose page 85

Readings

My yoga journey for self enlightenment includes reading and studying many books on the practice and philosophy of yoga and meditation. I have a very active account with Amazon. Books line my bookshelves, and a few are on my nightstand with favorite passages marked that guide me along a path of understanding and fulfillment and keep me from straying into self-doubt and self-righteousness.

Downey, Jessica. "The Dark Side of Meditation". *Yoga Journal.* May 2018: pp. 40-47.

Easwaran, Eknath (Introduced and translated by). The Bhagavad Gita. Tomales, CA: Nilgiri Press, 2007.

Flynn, E-RYT, RCYT, Lisa. Yoga for Children. Avon, MA: Adams Media, 2013.

Gates, Rolf and Kenison, Katrina. Meditations from the Mat: Daily Reflections on the Path of Yoga. New York: Anchor Books, 2002.

Gillian, MS, Lynea and Gillian, RYT, Jim. Yoga Calm for Children: Educating Heart, Mind, and Body. Portland, OR: Three Pebble Press, LLC, 2007.

Kaminoff, Leslie and Matthews, Amy. Yoga Anatomy (Second Edition). Champaign: IL, Human Kinetics, 2012.

Kempton, Sally. "Wisdom". *Yoga Journal.* December 201. p.57-58, 61-63.

Kiek, Michael, Boon, Brook, and DiTuro, Daniel. Hatha Yoga Illustrated. Champaign, IL: Human Kinetics, 2012.

Lasater, PH.D, PT, Judith. <u>Living Your Yoga: Finding the Spiritual in Everyday Life.</u> Berkley, CA: Rodmell Press, 2000.

Luck, Chanel. <u>Functional Anatomy For Flow</u>. Boston, MA: Radiant Yoga School, 2011.

Nhat Hanh, Thich and the Plum Village Community. <u>Planting Seeds: Practicing Mindfulness with Children</u>. Berkley, CA: Parallax Press, 2011.

Owen, Liz and Lebowitz Rossi, Holly. <u>Yoga for a Healthy Back: A Practical Guide to Developing Strength and Relieving Pain.</u> Boston, MA: Shambhala Publications, Inc., 2013.

Roach, Geshe Michael and McNally, Christie. <u>How Yoga Works</u>. Pompton Plains, NJ: Diamond Cutter Press, 2004.

Rountree, Sage. <u>The Athlete's Guide to Yoga: An Integrated Approach to Strength, Flexibility and Focus</u>. Boulder CO: Velo Press, 2008.

Satchidananda, Sri Swami (Translation and Commentary by). <u>The Yoga Sutras of Patanjali.</u> Buckingham, VA: Integral Yoga Publications, 2012.

State of Grace Yoga and Wellness Center. <u>Yoga Teacher Certification RYS 200 Registered Yoga School: State of Grace Yoga School Curriculum Manual.</u>

Svoboda, Dr. Robert E. <u>Ayurveda for Women: A Guide to Vitality and Health.</u> Rochester, VT: Healing Arts Press, 2000.

About the Author

Lisa Sherman, M. Ed., RYT 200, earned a Bachelor of Arts and a Master of Education degree in Elementary and Special Education from Rhode Island College and received Rhode Island certifications to work with students K-6 with special needs and regular education elementary level students. She later completed the study necessary to pass the National Board examination to become a National Board-Certified Teacher in 2004.

Since in 1991, Lisa has taught children at the Bradley School, a residential psychiatric program run by Bradly Hospital, court ordered adolescent offenders in a private residential treatment center, young disabled children in the public schools, and for the last 15 years has taught regular second-grade students in the West Warwick public schools.

Lisa began attending yoga classes in 2010, and in 2013 began her 200-hour yoga instructor's training program at the State of Grace Yoga and Wellness Center.

She has since taken yoga classes in yoga assists, yoga for anxiety and depression, seasonal yoga, and yoga for children.

Lisa continues to practice yoga for herself at home three to four times a week and most Sunday mornings at State of Grace. She teaches yoga in her school for teachers and with community programs.

Lisa and her husband enjoy sailing and skiing together. They live at home with their cat while their daughter, Catherine, attends Worcester Polytechnic Institute as a junior and is looking toward graduate work in computational biology.

ॐ

www.ingramcontent.com/pod-product-compliance
Lightning Source LLC
LaVergne TN
LVHW021457080426
835509LV00018B/2318